Ben Mckelvey is an author, journalist and editor from Bondi, Sydney. Ben's books have won the Australian Independent Book Award for non-fiction, an Australian Book Industry Award and the Nib Military History Prize, and have been shortlisted in the Victorian and Queensland Premier's Literary Awards and for the Les Carlyon Literary Prize. Ben has been the editor of *Mr Jones, Sports&Style* and *Juice* magazines and worked at the *Sydney Morning Herald* as the Senior Feature Writer. Ben has been embedded with the Australian Defence Force in Timor-Leste and Iraq, and has worked independently in Iran, Lebanon and Afghanistan.

Also by Ben Mckelvey

Find Fix Finish

Mosul

The Commando

Valerie Taylor: An Adventurous Life

Born to Fight

Songs of a War Boy

a memoir of stroke,
heart attack and remaking

a scar is also skin

Ben Mckelvey

hachette AUSTRALIA
Published in Australia and New Zealand in 2023
by Hachette Australia
(an imprint of Hachette Australia Pty Limited)
Gadigal Country, Level 17, 207 Kent Street, Sydney, NSW 2000
www.hachette.com.au

Hachette Australia acknowledges and pays our respects to the past, present and future Traditional Owners and Custodians of Country throughout Australia and recognises the continuation of cultural, spiritual and educational practices of Aboriginal and Torres Strait Islander peoples. Our head office is located on the lands of the Gadigal people of the Eora Nation.

A catalogue record for this work is available from the National Library of Australia

ISBN: 978 0 7336 4504 4 (paperback)

Cover design by Christabella Designs
Cover illustration courtesy of Janusz Jurek
Typeset in 12/20pt Sabon LT Std by Kirby Jones
Printed and bound in Australia by McPherson's Printing Group

The paper this book is printed on is certified against the Forest Stewardship Council® Standards. McPherson's Printing Group holds FSC® chain of custody certification SA-COC-005379. FSC® promotes environmentally responsible, socially beneficial and economically viable management of the world's forests.

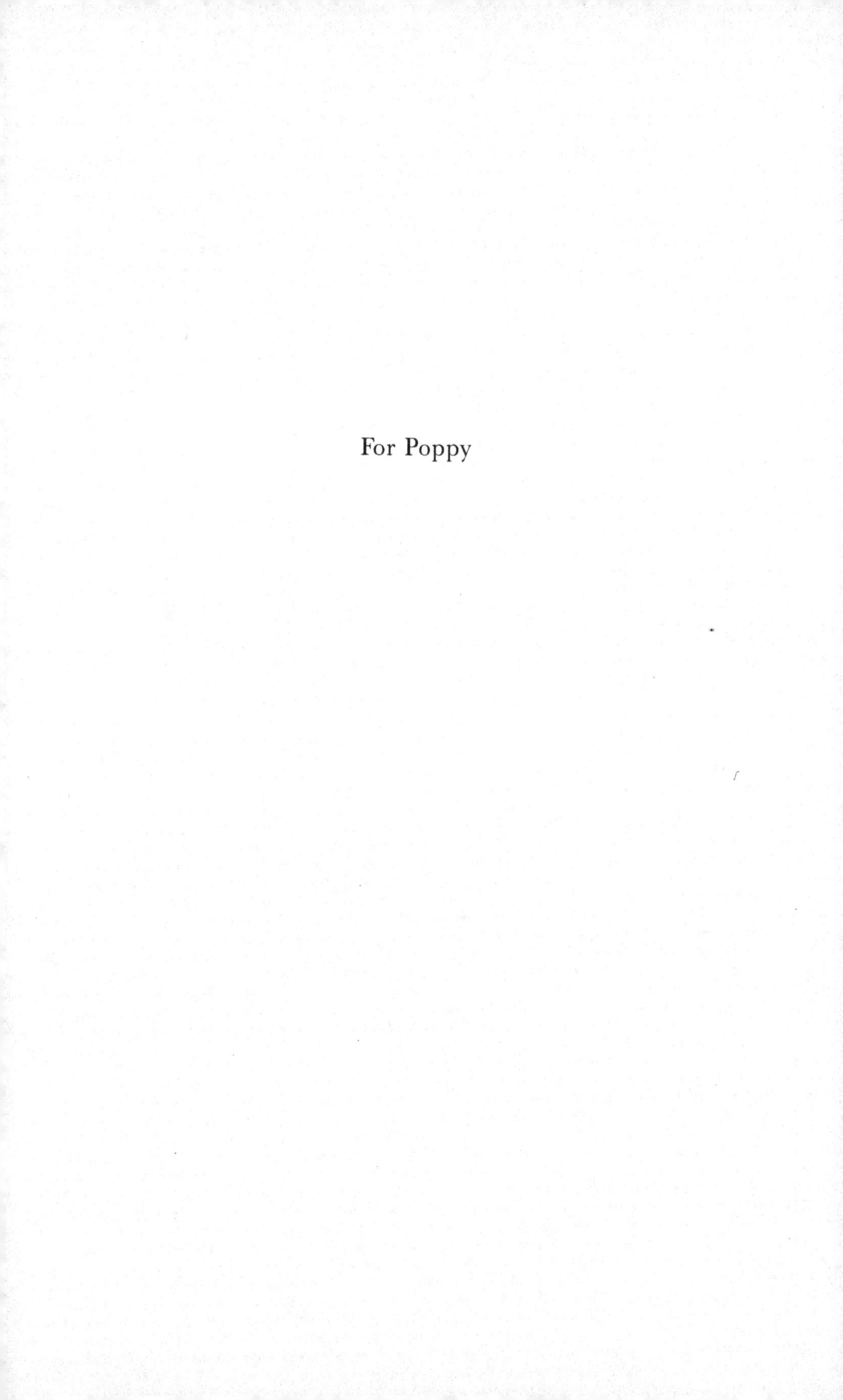

For Poppy

Yes, I will be thy priest, and build a fane
In some untrodden region of my mind,
Where branched thoughts, new grown with pleasant pain,
Instead of pines shall murmur in the wind

John Keats, *Ode to Psyche*

Nothing happens in the world?
Are you out of your fucking mind?

Charlie Kaufman, *Adaptation*

CONTENTS

Prologue		1
Part I		5
Chapter 1	The Snap	7
Chapter 2	Morning Light	21
Chapter 3	On Neuroplasticity	35
Chapter 4	Memory, Childhood	45
Chapter 5	Vertigo	63
Chapter 6	A Feast in the East	85
Chapter 7	A Scar is Also Skin	119
Chapter 8	The Bad War	143
Part II		157
Chapter 9	Born to Fight	159
Chapter 10	Songs of a War Boy	181
Chapter 11	On Addiction, On Archie Roach	209
Part III		229
Chapter 12	Happiness is a Warm Gun	231
Chapter 13	Externalities	247

Chapter 14 And There You Were 273
Chapter 15 Sunrise, Sunset 287

Epilogue 299

Select Sources 305
Acknowledgements 309

prologue

As I write these words, I can see my dad on the screen of my phone, propped up to the left of my computer. He's asleep on a bed in the front room of his cottage in Mandurah, Western Australia. I'm in a room probably designed as a closet but now serving as my office in our apartment in Bondi.

Dad was dying slowly for a couple of years, and now I'm watching him die quickly. I'm not with him because I'm writing this during the waning end of the Covid panic and Western Australia still has a hard border with the rest of the country.

I'm angry that I can't be with my dad, but mostly I feel sadness. It's a sadness that I know will never completely disappear. It'll be folded into me, like spice in a simmering dish.

Around Dad are his final loves: his partner, Marlene, and my sister, Laura, with pictures of her daughters, my nieces, nearby. There's very faint music on his stereo – Buddy Holly – and I can also just hear the football commentary coming from a telly he bought at K-Mart. Real football, as he calls it. The football of Dad's English youth.

Dad is mostly sleeping now, except in a few instances when he raises just above the consciousness threshold. He's not supposed to cross that threshold anymore. We're past that. The goal is to keep him as comfortable as possible, and consciousness is no longer compatible with his comfort. Nurses come into view twice a day to make sure Dad transitions out of this world with as much dignity and ease as possible.

It hurts to write these words, and will hurt to reread them when my dad is no longer in this world. I have to get them down though.

There's a lot I don't understand about my dad. I always loved him, and he me, but he lived what looked to me like a puzzle of a life. My dad is probably one of the reasons I'm a writer, and he's one of two reasons I'm writing this book.

The other reason I'm writing this book is to the right of my computer screen. On a small plastic monitor, splayed out on a mattress, is the image of my sleeping six-month-old daughter, Poppy. If I stop typing, I hear a faint, soporific symphony: the rising and falling of Dad's snoring through the phone speakers to my left and the consistent hum of Poppy's white-noise machine to my right.

There is some kind of balance in front of me, with the start and end of life either side of my computer. I can feel joy and sadness as I look between the screens, but not balance. If I am honest, I feel a rising and familiar panic. My thoughts are disordered.

I sat down today in the hope that I could write my way to some kind of balance or shape. That often happens when you write a book. When you sit in front of a blank page, infinite permutations offer themselves and a storyteller chooses the ones that suggest signal through noise, creating meaning from chaos. Everything that's printed is the story. Anything that isn't printed, isn't anything at all.

I've managed to bring shape and balance to the story of other people's lives, and now I'll try to do it with my life, in this moment of sadness and happiness and pain and disorder. In this moment of mental peril.

Lives are easy when there is order. Lives are interesting when there's disorder. Most of us move from one to the other and back again, sometimes even creating a state of disorder, because it's in these disordered times that our lives, and we ourselves, change.

In the same way that we sometimes burn land to promote regrowth and ecological balance, we occasionally bring disorder to our lives in the hope of growth or change. Sometimes unmanaged fires roar through our lives too. Sometimes we have set the fires ourselves, and some are acts of god. These fires offer growth and change as well as death and destruction.

This book is about these kinds of fires. It is about change and damage, triumph and loss. It is about my life, and it starts on 16 July 2004, a day like no other I've had. It was the day in which my brain, mind and life changed, radically and forever.

Part I

Chapter 1

the snap

I'm twenty-seven years old, fit, young, pretty happy and also lazy and cynical. I work at a large circulation men's magazine, *Ralph*, loosely modelled on a very good counterculture British magazine called *Loaded*. The magazine I work for is not counterculture and is not *Loaded*, but I don't really care. I mostly like the people I work with and the lifestyle the job affords me.

Everyone at the magazine drinks for free, and we drink a lot. We go to gigs for free, see movies for free and are often flown around the world to do this or that.

Mostly nonsense. I have a girlfriend, who also works in magazines. I don't earn much, but I don't have much ambition so there's a comfortable equanimity at play.

Though I write all day, I'm not yet a writer. My output could be capably described as 'content', which also describes the innards of a service station hot dog and an Ikea bean bag.

I can't remember arriving late to work on 16 July 2004, but I probably did. I would have gossiped and joked through the morning, perhaps replying to some emails and ignoring others. What work was done at *Ralph* was usually done in the afternoon. I took an early lunch hour with some of the other editorial staff, heading for the gym across the road, under the Catholic Club.

I was in the gym when it happened. I was hitting the heavy bag: straights to the top of the bag, hooks to the middle, bashing at imaginary kidneys. I felt good – free and young and strong – but inside of me a blood clot, which had developed in my hip days or weeks before, had broken free from its vascular mooring and was wending its way through my bloodstream and up my body.

As a digital timer above a mirror counted down the seconds, I watched my form as I punched. The timer counted down to zero and then dinged three times. I shook the lactic acid from my arms. A large fan blessed me with cool air. My t-shirt was matted against my chest and my neck and face were hot and crimson. I felt great.

I slowly shadowboxed as 2Pac's song 'California Love', one of my favourites, came over the stereo. The timer's chime struck twice and I was at it again. As I'd been trained to do, I breathed out sharply as I punched, creating abdominal pressure and transverse force into my glove.

Psht-phst.

THWACK-THWACK.

I would find out later that this is called the Valsalva Manoeuvre. I would also find out later that a by-product of this manoeuvre can be an unusual haemodynamics, with blood travelling in an unusual direction in the body. Unusual but almost always harmless. Almost always.

The clot from my hip smuggled itself up to my chest and then gushed into my heart with some blood, entering the cardiac chambers through my aortic valve. My heart pumped, sending oxygenated blood through my chest, neck and up towards my brain. The clot followed.

I kept hammering away at the bag.

Left, right, hook-hook.

Psht, psht, psht-psht.

I worked and boxed and sweated and the clot jerked around the vascular highways of my brain with each heartbeat, before wedging itself into a tight blood vessel a few inches behind my mouth. The clot was stuck, the vessel was clogged and blood that should be feeding a section of my brain with oxygen was trapped. The cells in my brain started to choke and die. My mind started to change.

I had been rapping in my head as I boxed, until the words of 'California Love' blew away as though they were dust. Soon only the bouncing beat remained. Butterflies waltzed in my vision. A splotchy thought was in my head, one that I could only later define.

Strange.

That thought continued as I searched for the words to the song that rolled on without me. I couldn't catch any of them in the front of my consciousness, not even the words 'California' or 'Love'.

Strange.

I stopped boxing and pulled my gloves off. I spun my wraps out. I was confused. I knew this song well.

Strange.

I stood naked in a cold shower. The waltzing butterflies in front of my eyes became kites of spotted light and colour.

Strange.

I managed to clothe myself and fill my gym bag. I walked out onto the street.

Strange.

The street seemed familiar but I didn't know where to go.

Strange.

A face appeared in front of me, also flushed red from gym work. It's a familiar face yet there's no name associated with it.

Strange.

The familiar face recognised me. He was a friend. I knew I should say something, but there was nothing to say. I didn't have any words accessible to me. I tried anyway. Something came out of my mouth. Verbal sludge. I understood the language of my friend's face.

Panic.

Something was wrong. I tried again to say what was happening and again I couldn't. I could tell my friend was shocked and scared. I could tell he was scared for me. Another emotion surged through my brain like a tide.

Sad.

I didn't know then what I was losing, but I knew it was a lot. I was disconnected, so much so that I couldn't account for exactly what and who I was disconnected from. The disconnection hurt very badly.

Sad.

Tears grew in my eyes then built and burst. They streamed down my cheeks. I looked at this friend, this stranger. I shrugged, palms upturned. The taste of my tears as they ran into the corners of my smile is a memory that endures.

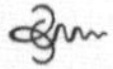

For the next hour or so, I was at a medical centre on Pitt Street in Sydney, staring blankly at an irritated receptionist and a medical consent form. I was told later she was convinced my brain was addled on ice.

The strong emotional journey my brain had gone through in the first minutes after the event was likely mostly over. I say likely, because I only have grabs of memory after leaving the gym.

In the medical centre, I remember the traffic outside, a sign with red letters on a white background, and my friend pleading for an ambulance. I also remember one strong emotion.

I'm not sure I can exactly explain the nomenclature of the emotion but it's the feeling I used to have when, as a little boy, I'd be in bed in a darkened room with heavy skin and a fevered forehead, and I'd hear life continuing outside – the postie pushing letters into the letterbox, kids on their bikes laughing, Dad collecting his things as he prepared to go to work.

Jealousy, FOMO, envy – I suppose it was all those things but none exactly describe the feeling. Can disconnection be an emotion? If so, it was that. This was something I would feel many times, and in varying degrees, in the weeks and months to come.

I was eventually deposited at the emergency ward of St Vincent's Hospital, close to Kings Cross. The controlled rush of too much work and too few medical staff was all around me. The rush was exacerbated as a junkie was brought in, screaming something I either couldn't hear or couldn't understand. I was led to a partitioned area that served as an examination room and there I waited, alone.

The admitting physician arrived. My heart rate and blood pressure seemed fine, I had no pain nor mobility issues and there seemed to be no issues with my coordination – I was able to follow a pen with my eyes and mimic movements with my fingers when prompted. I could take instruction after charades and prompting, but I couldn't understand any verbal instructions. I was almost wholly disconnected from language.

The doctor decided that something was going on – probably not the drug reaction that was suspected – but I appeared to be stable. He decided that I was not in imminent danger of dying and I found out later that he issued an initial diagnosis of infection in my cerebrospinal fluid.

I was taken to a corner of emergency and there I watched a silent television. The news came on and I saw a house on fire, a uniformed policeman behind a microphone, traffic seen from the air, swimmers in a pool, a medal ceremony. I tried so hard to force a narrative onto the images I saw that I developed a migraine.

A nurse came and took some of my blood. I smiled blandly. Time passed, but I couldn't really parse how much time. Some friends arrived and I realised they'd finished their workday and it was evening. They would be going home or out for dinner. I would not be. I had that disconnected feeling again.

I knew my friends' faces, but not their names. Another doctor came in and started speaking to me. As he spoke, I smiled and nodded in the way a toddler might when being spoken at: understanding the cadence of the language but little of the content. I still couldn't speak nor comprehend well what was going on. A friend persisted with me until I understood that I would be taken to a ward where they'd administer a spinal tap, also known as a lumbar puncture, so they could draw some cerebrospinal fluid and test it.

I remember the smell of the lumbar puncture – acrid and medical – and the sound: the scrape of needle against spine. I remember a doctor, young and serious. I remember his sweater, very colourful like a Ken Done painting and clearly knitted by a loved one. I remember smiling like a dolt and I also vividly remember a shining moment of hope.

My friends were talking and joking over me as I lay on my hospital bed. I didn't really understand their words, but tried to keep up as best I could so I would smile or chuckle, nod or shake my head when appropriate. I found myself staring at one friend's t-shirt. Across it was one word, with illustrations around it. Through the idle chat of my friends, I focused on the shirt's words and pictures with intensity. I couldn't read the words, but I understood the pictures. There were mountains, snow-capped, and there were black bears. I tried to read the word, I managed to read a letter. The first letter: V. I put the sound of the letter in my mind and rolled it around as you might roll a hard candy in your mouth.

I managed to pull some other letters from the t-shirt and put those in my mind also. I tried to put the letters together, and then the sounds together. I added the pictures.

V-V… black bears … *an-an* … snowy mountains … *V-V-Van … Vancouver!*

The word on the shirt was Vancouver. I said it out loud, but quietly. I remember an instinct not to be embarrassed. I tried to put together a sentence explaining my revelation. None came, so I didn't say anything.

It felt good knowing that word. Hopeful.

That night, I was given a bed on a ward. I was already getting better, and I was understanding more and being able to say more. I was still confused by most sentences but questions like 'Do you want some tea?' could be answered with 'Yes, please' or 'No, thank you'.

In the relative quiet and dark of the hospital night, I understood that the doctors believed a virus was affecting me. That was something I thought I could handle. I'd had viruses before, and they'd run a predictable path: sickness and then less sickness and then little sickness and then no sickness. This incident I was experiencing had roughly run that path also and I was already in the less-sickness stage.

After finding that my cerebrospinal fluid was normal, and after a CT scan and then an MRI scan, it was decided that I hadn't suffered a virus but a stroke.

This was a few days after my admission. I don't remember exactly when I was first given this information, but I remember doctors saying the word 'stroke' to me when listing the things that probably didn't happen to me, and then when listing things that may have happened to me, and eventually it was described as fact.

An older doctor came to me one day, with a group of studious-looking men and women who were all younger than I was. They crowded around me while the older doctor rattled off a long string of descriptors to his students. The word 'ischaemic stroke' was wedged in the middle. As he was about to move on to the next bed, I touched his arm.

'Stroke?' I asked.

'Yes.'

'I had a stroke?'

'Yes.'

'You sure?'

Flipping through the file at the end of my bed, he hummed until he found what he was looking for.

'Yes. Stroke,' he said.

He patted my hand and moved on.

At the best of times, it's difficult to understand who's in charge in a hospital, and which information is most important. It's even harder when in a state of shock, illness or, in my case, aphasia: a language, communications and cognitive disorder that was the main symptom of my stroke.

I had a lot of questions, some of which I managed to articulate to my primary doctor. The question I most wanted to know was whether my aphasia would be permanent. He told me that question could best be answered by my neurologist. When the neurologist came, he told me he didn't know. He told me it can't be known. He said they couldn't identify what had happened but there had been an occlusion or vascular blockage in the left side of my brain, which was where, for most people, language and computational reasoning is primarily processed.

He said he thought that this blockage starved parts of the left side of my brain of blood and, more importantly, the oxygen that was in my blood. Without oxygen, the cells started to die. The occlusion eventually resolved itself, and here we are.

I asked about those parts of my brain that were damaged. Were those dead cells dead forever? He said they were, but also that that didn't mean that the tasks those cells performed could never again be performed. Stroke victims, especially young stroke victims, could often attain normal levels of language and comprehension after aphasic episodes.

Could ... often?

In the days and weeks that came after my admission, this neurologist, who was diligent and intelligent, seemed only to have minimal interest in my recovery because, in his view, it was rapid. He was more concerned with identifying why I'd suffered a stroke and whether I was about to have another one. I quickly gleaned he was not in charge of neurological nuance, then slowly gleaned that no one would (or could) be in charge of neurological nuance but the patient. As soon as I could speak and read some words, I was no longer in a state of aphasia, according to my doctors. As far as they were concerned, I was recovered or recovering.

The doctors' primary concern was the cause of my stroke. Everything else was a lesser concern. When the lumbar puncture leaked cerebrospinal fluid and gave me migraines during the day, it wasn't considered much of an issue by my doctors. The nausea I suffered from the morphine issued to lessen my headaches wasn't thought about much either. Those were paint scratches on a spluttering jet engine. Twenty-seven-year-olds with no prior conditions generally didn't have strokes.

After a week in hospital, I hadn't recovered. Not really. Not fully. I couldn't speak with any fluidity. I couldn't read much nor could I speak very well. I couldn't concentrate. I could order a meal and read a label, but I couldn't read a book or tell a multi-stage joke.

I must have been hiding my aphasia well, though, because people kept adding to a stack of magazines and books next to my bed. The books were daunting but in a quiet moment I decided to have a look at the first page of a short novel called *Intimacy* by Hanif Kureishi.

I sometimes forced my way onto page two of the book, but there I had to admit I didn't know what was going on. No matter how slowly I read, I couldn't put information – who a character was, where they were and what they were doing – in my head so I could move on to the next phase of action. It was like attempting to put shoes on for a walk, but endlessly catching your socks on your toes.

I knew Hanif Kureishi was a heady author, and even though *Intimacy* was short and written using simple language, I thought perhaps it was an ambitious place to be getting back on the reading road. I tried some of the magazines on my stack, but I couldn't read anything in those either.

I despaired. I knew my brain had changed permanently, and if my brain had changed then I had changed. I had issues with language but I wondered what other neurological functions had been impaired and what parts of me were now gone: cognitively, emotionally and essentially.

Chapter 2

morning light

The days in hospital were full, even the days when I was just in the business of waiting. There were always doctors who I needed to see, who were rumoured to be on their way, and there were often tests that were purported to be happening. There were nurses coming to check on my bowels and cannulas to be replaced, and there were well-meaning visitors and the offer of inedible meals. There were also migraines and the morphine and nausea, so during the daytime there usually wasn't too much opportunity to ruminate.

Things were different at night, however. Hospitals generally clear out when the sun sets, except for a skeleton staff and, of course, the inpatients.

For some reason, my nausea and migraines sometimes abated at night and my mind was relatively clear. I often spent time thinking how an inability to read and write was probably going to be an impediment to my magazine career, even as an editor at *Ralph.* There was a more fundamental question resonating in my head, however: was I the same person who I had been previously? Did I have an issue with articulating my memories, thoughts and emotions or had those memories, thoughts and emotions themselves been compromised?

I didn't speak to anyone about this while I was in hospital, perhaps because I didn't have the words to properly explain myself, or perhaps because no one had brought the subject up and in hospital it's quite poor form to complain to the people around you about speculations, especially when, all things considered, you've already been quite fortunate. After all, I could walk and talk.

But that question was always in my mind, at least at night.

I remember those hospital nights as long. I'd been a night owl, usually going to bed well after midnight, and my circadian rhythms were at odds with the cadence of hospital life, which was built around geriatric patients.

Many of the patients on my ward were older men who fell straight to sleep as soon as the lights on the ward dimmed at eight. They filled the night with cacophonous snores and the odd loud fart. Some of the patients on my ward stayed awake, cranking their tiny personal speakers to the maximum volume as they watched the ABC.

Sometimes I also turned on the little cathode-ray tube TV above my bed and pressed the tinny plastic speaker against my ear. In the first week in hospital, I surfed endlessly through the five channels as I thought about something else.

In my second week in hospital, however, I surfed my way over to SBS to find that Stanley Kubrick's film *Paths of Glory* was about to start as part of a Kubrick retrospective, running all week.

That retrospective made my nights in hospital far easier, and also the days, as I had something to look forward to.

The television I watched the films on was perhaps fourteen inches diagonally, the screen curved and broadcasting in fuzzy standard definition. The speaker was comparable to the kind that greets you when entering a McDonalds drive-through. And yet, in my mind, the sights and sounds from those films are impeccable and immersive, and attached to a feeling of exhilaration. In hospital, my mind was soaring with possibilities.

I was relieved to know I could still feel something when I watched, and some time in the second week in hospital, I found that I could still connect to my feelings when I read.

One night I picked up an omnibus of Harvey Pekar's autobiographical comic books, *American Splendor*, and was sucked into the minutia of his seemingly unremarkable life as a twice-divorced Jewish file clerk in Cleveland.

While the books are funny, there are no jokes. The stories are about the nuance of life, the grain and texture that makes us feel our days as they go by. I was engaged with the stories, not just intellectually but emotionally.

In reading *American Splendor*, I didn't only have shoes and socks on, I was walking, running, jumping. This is what I'd always loved, ever since I was a little kid. I loved to read, I loved to watch, I loved to understand other people and the world through a medium.

I was often troubled by how quickly I'd be left behind, in conversation and context. When my friends and girlfriend spoke in hospital, it was sometimes as though I was hearing them speak in another language, and I would desperately try to grab a word or phrase that could drag me into the conversation. When I spoke, I saw in their faces the polite patience people employ when listening to a non-English speaker. I knew that sometimes they were waiting for me to come to my confused point so we could all move along.

I grew scared of being left behind, in conversations and in life. Even only after two weeks, it felt like life was continuing without me, and would continue to happen without me.

I feared that the life in front of me might be less meaningful than the one behind me. I might understand less and feel less, although I was probably confusing the broader numbing effects of life in hospital with the specific and personal effect of the brain damage I had suffered.

I had always been an over-thinker. Whenever I'd battled a clouding surplus of thought in one area of my life, I often tried to think my way to clarity. I then believed that only thought could conquer thought. That wasn't going to work here. I was over-thinking at a time when I was least equipped for it.

I know now that I also use diversion when I start over-thinking. That wasn't working after my stroke until Harvey Pekar and Stanley Kubrick came on to my ward. They brought diversion, but they also brought hope that while my life going forward might be different to my old life, it might not be lesser. As I read and watched, I thought that perhaps my capacity for language would be affected but not my capacity for feeling.

Harvey Pekar and Stanley Kubrick had a lot to say to me, most importantly: 'You can still connect deeply' and

'Regardless of whether you'll write again, or even read a novel, there is marrow left in the bone that is life.'

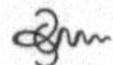

I'd been in hospital a couple of weeks and my migraines and nausea had stopped. I'd stopped taking morphine and I'd been disconnected from my heart monitor and drip. I was getting better. I'd stopped thinking so much as well. I read comics, watched movies and, with the prodding and testing over, I was ready to go home.

One night around this time, a man died on the ward. I woke in the dark early morning to a minor commotion of nurses, doctors and crash carts. The commotion gave way to snoring and the slow steady beeps of machines around me. Orderlies arrived and I saw a body being taken away on a gurney.

I fell asleep again and woke with the ward, which was unaffected by the loss of the man. Breakfast came. Nurses chatted. Old men stared out the window. The day unfolded.

The man who had died was just one of the men on the ward – I wasn't even sure which one. He was probably lonely (only a fraction of the old men received visitors) and probably not expecting for his life to end when it did.

It was such an anonymous, matter-of-fact occurrence. And that was what chilled me.

Instead of thinking about death and spiralling into over-thinking, my mind gave me visceral wants. I wanted a beer and a second beer. I wanted fat, salt and sugar. I wanted to blast Queens of the Stone Age, get laid and take a big shit in my own toilet. I really wanted to get the hell out of hospital.

I wasn't receiving any treatments, nor was I undergoing any tests, but my doctors were still reluctant to release me without identifying the source of the stroke. Eventually one of my doctors told me they were going to convene a 'council' where all my data would be presented to a large gathering of specialists in the hope of identifying a specific diagnosis.

After settling on a broad-spectrum diagnosis of 'unidentified predisposition to thrombus', I was finally prepped for discharge. I was visited by a physiotherapist, an occupational therapist and a speech and language therapist, which was the standard bookend to any hospital admission after a stroke. The physiotherapist had no work to do, nor the speech therapist.

I'd been looking forward to seeing the occupational therapist because I'd asked numerous doctors when we were going to start treatment that would help bring me back to myself – that was what I considered a full recovery, with my thoughts and language as they had been before. I was never satisfied with the answers I got and there didn't seem to be anyone who was going to be helping me return to me, except this occupational therapist.

My hopes were too high and I was disappointed after her visit. That wasn't an indictment of her or her field, but on my wildly unrealistic expectations. I wanted a lot. I knew I wasn't thinking as I used to nor using language as I had before. It was taking me a long time to explain things that I knew should be able to be explained quickly. I knew my brain was often stuck with its first attempt at a word, unable to find a second or third example once a first had been lodged in my mind. I knew I was often mixing up my tenses, mistaking today for yesterday, and before and after, but only in speech, not in my mind. I knew I meant tomorrow.

I wanted to know why, even when I had all the required parts of a sentence or paragraph in my mind, I couldn't assemble them properly. I wanted to know why there were concepts I understood, but that I had seemingly lost the words for (I still struggle to find the word 'codependent' when I need it for some reason). I wanted to know why sometimes I'd see an empty word space approaching and I'd be stuck, mid-sentence of mid-thought.

(I built a defence against this – telling my friends and family that I was just going to stick the word 'cornflakes' in front of my mind and say that instead of the incorrect word).

I expected my occupational therapist to tell a story, arriving with CT and MRI scans in the way an orthopaedic specialist might, identifying a tear or a break, and then give me strategies for recovery and reconstruction.

What was my issue? Was it memory, cognition, language, a mix? I was keen to know.

Instead she came in with flash cards of clip art and shapes and colours. Could I identify this? It's a sailboat. And this colour? Green. And this shape? It's a circle. I asked her a few of my questions about language and emotion and she told me that these questions were a little outside of her field. I was disheartened. She continued with her flash cards. Of course I could identify what was on the cards. This was an umbrella, a pentagon, a wave.

'This?' she asked.

Of course, it was a … circle. No. Not a circle. It had straight lines so it was a … circle? No, it was pointy. Circles aren't pointy, it's a … circle. Fuck me. No, not a circle but a square. Not quite a square …

'It's half a square,' I said.

'Nearly!' she enthused.

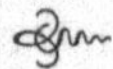

I was discharged from hospital, went home and resumed my life, essentially. I couldn't read easily yet, and I still used the word 'cornflakes' for missing words, but from the outside it seemed no other aspect of my life had been significantly affected.

From the inside, though, things were definitely different. If I allowed myself any quietude, there was no getting away from the fact that my brain had changed and so had I. I didn't want a brain that had changed and I didn't want a different life, so the answer to that problem was to refuse any moments of quietude that may intrude.

I wasn't sick and wasn't even really convalescing, so I just filled my life up with the joys of Sydney for a few weeks until, with an aching liver, clothes that smelled like an ashtray (I was an ardent non-smoker, but the indoor smoking ban in Sydney was still a couple of years away) and ringing ears, I returned to work.

Initially I did tasks that required the least amount of English comprehension and composition – captioning, interviewing glamour models and personalities to be used as Q&A text, and writing short movie and music reviews. Then, perhaps four months after the stroke, I attempted my first long-form piece of writing.

The story required me to go to Willowbank Raceway in Queensland and write a piece about a family who had made money in the crane business, and had put that money into a drag-racing team, which they owned and operated. After returning to Sydney, I spent weeks arranging and rearranging text and quotes that couldn't have been more than two thousand words.

I convinced myself that there was sense in the document that I'd created; that I'd introduced people, a place and milieu and, through description and quotes, I'd taken the reader on a journey.

What I'd written was unreadable gabble.

The filing process in our office was that when you had finished a story, you'd move the first draft of it onto the office server so it could be subedited, and then a printed copy would be left on the magazine editor's desk. My desk had a direct line of sight to the editor and I watched him pick my feature up and slump deeper and deeper into his chair as he read.

I felt my face flush. Days after the stroke (and before it was known I'd had a stroke), a card arrived from the magazine and the editor had written: 'Entire feature written in Mckelvey gibberish? By crikey, I think it may work.' I could see in his posture now – head in his hands –

that he knew an entire feature written in gibberish was not going to work.

It was depressing, but the absurdity and awkwardness of the situation also amused me. The magazine was, at the time, overstaffed with some odd characters, so I figured I'd probably just be the illiterate editor for a while.

'This is Gourmet Gav, he dresses like a chef sometimes. This is Chris our staff writer and, no, I don't know why he's bleeding. And here's Ben, our features editor. He can't read or write.'

If I didn't get better, I figured I'd just find something else to do. As I said, I wasn't ambitious, nor did I have any expectation that I'd be a good writer. I aspired to be a good writer, but that aspiration wasn't attached to much belief.

I do wonder now whether this lack of ambition was a defence mechanism, one that was developed at high school and then dusted off after my brain was damaged. I wonder now, too, whether this attitude was part of the culture at the magazine I worked on. I do know, however, that I was relatively unbothered by my inabilities. Those months after the stroke were hazy, perhaps due to the amount I was drinking or perhaps due to the brain damage I'd suffered, but some moments and thoughts are crystallised, and I vividly remember wondering why I was unbothered by my disordered and almost unusable copy.

I figured that it must be that I didn't want more in life than to drink for free and see movies and fly around the world. If I had to pay for those privileges, it'd be a shame, but almost anything else I might do would likely pay better than working at a magazine so it'd work itself out.

Winston Churchill once said: 'Never let a good crisis go to waste', which is exactly what I was doing.

Thankfully, this crisis was far from done.

Chapter 3

on neuroplasticity

Neuroplasticity essentially describes the human brain's ability to adapt to the environment it finds itself in. It's something I owe my life and work to, but I'm not the only one.

There's no way of overstating how important neuroplasticity is to us as a species and to each of us individually. If our genes are the hand we're dealt in the poker game of life, neuroplasticity is the way we play that hand. It's the post-natal architecture of how we move through the world, how we think and feel. It's the living history of our lives, expressed as abilities and emotions.

When brain degeneration comes, through damage or age, neuroplasticity is also what gives us a chance to stay ourselves.

Without neuroplasticity, I would have stayed the confused mess I was when I walked out of the boxing gym, unable to speak or even access the names of friends and family.

During the stroke, I suffered brain damage, which was noticeable in MRI imagery. This damage resulted in effects such as my sudden aphasia, or loss of language. The tissue in my brain that was being used to process language was dead and would never be regenerated, but that didn't mean that my capacity to process language was lost forever. Instead, that function was restored through the process of neuronal rerouting and reorganisation. That is neuroplasticity.

Imagine a bridge bisecting a busy modern city with superbly planned and well-maintained infrastructure. If that bridge is destroyed, does that mean no one will ever be able to go from one side of the city to the other? Not necessarily. The first time you approach the bridge, you may be stuck in an almighty traffic jam and may not get to your destination that day, but there will be other ways, and other days, to get where you want to go. Neuroplasticity, essentially the Google Maps of the brain, will find that new route. And not only that, with repeated use, neuroplasticity can turn bush tracks to dirt roads, dirt roads to bitumen and then bitumen into superhighways.

The human brain is uniquely complex and uniquely malleable. There are somewhere between 70 and 100 billion neurons in each human brain, and these neurons connect with each other through chemical junctions called synapses, of which, in each brain, there may be hundreds of trillions. The number of potential unique neuronal processes or brain states is truly incredible.

We achieve only a tiny fraction of those potential brain states in our lifetime. There are neurons, synapses and brain states that are hard-coded into certain essential functions (breathing comes to mind), but that still leaves a vast amount of neurons, synapses and brain states that can freelance. What they do depends on the environments we find ourselves in, and what we do in those environments.

The scale of the human ability to match brain states with environment-dependent use is unique and has given us abilities only our species has managed. One of those abilities is language.

Every person's journey into language is an epic one, and it starts even before we are born.

A 2009 French scientific study found that babies start to learn the French language even before birth. The study found that, even immediately after being born, French babies cry in the 'melody' of the language of their parents, with those cries being more likely to rise in tone, matching the tendency of the French language. The study found that German babies' cries fall in tone, matching German sentences. From their findings, the study asserted that the child starts to learn their language in utero.

My mother was speaking to me from the moment I entered the world at Canberra Hospital, with Dad's voice coming a little later, when he returned from a café nearby. Every time they spoke to me, my brain changed a little as it attempted to mimic and understand what they were saying.

Baby utterances became words and, like most of us, 'ma' and 'da' were the first words I spoke. Ma. Da. Nouns. Those figures in view keeping me safe, warm and fed. The journey of words had begun.

My brain continued to change so that soon the squiggles on a page could become words. The houses I grew up in always had books, and children's books were a part of my every day, even when I was a baby. Every time I was read to, my brain was then linking words to object, actions to words and picking up syntax, story structure, grammar and culture, as well as creating an ability to project emotion through text.

When I'm asked how someone becomes a writer, there's only one answer: read. To be writer, you have to read, as much as you can and as widely as you can. The truth of the matter, though, is that starting to read now may help but to be a writer, you probably have to have read as a child, as so many of the brain structures required to write are developed in the vital, fertile, early years of your life.

Throughout childhood, the human brain massively overproduces synapses, creating incredible possibilities of neuronal linking. Then the brain slowly sheds those synapses if they're not being incorporated into neuronal processes. Known in neuroscience as the 'use it or lose it' development periods, it's an essential process in the development of language skills, reading, and writing. It's also a large part of why learning a language is difficult later in life, when there isn't a synaptic surplus to exploit when trying to get your head around new words, new grammar and new sounds. It's also the reason why when most people learn a new language as an adult, they will never be able to speak that language without the intrusion of a mother tongue accent.

It's not only skill and functions that are affected by neuroplasticity, though, but also the brain's higher functions like emotion, philosophy, art appreciation and spiritual expression.

The last synaptic stacking and shedding periods in a child's brain starts at about age five and ends somewhere around eighteen. It happens in the prefrontal cortex, an area in the brain that is linked to higher cognitive functions and the expression of a personality and identity.

The fact that this neuronal overproduction and shedding coincides with the pre-teen and teen years undoubtedly contributes to the fact that many of us have a life-long appreciation for the art and music of our youth, no matter how questionable it may have been.

The mechanism of neuroplasticity does not end with the 'use it or lose it' development period though. We continue to learn and change throughout our lives and every brain stays 'elastic' in varying degrees until death. But this mechanism can degrade over time. I consider myself lucky that I suffered a stroke at the age I did.

During and immediately after my stroke, when I was trying to speak and then to read, the neuronal processes that developed during the 'use it to lose it' phase in my childhood were engaged. This was like turning an ignition unattached to an engine. Some parts of my brain that were used in the neuronal processes I had developed for language simply were no longer there.

If neuroplasticity didn't exist, then the state of confusion and aphasia I was in when I was first delivered to the hospital is the state I would have stayed in, condemned to a maddening traffic jam of a life. Thanks to neuroplasticity, however, another set of neuronal processes emerged. My brain searched out new bush tracks that could eventually become highways.

An MRI of my brain taken just after the stroke showed noticeable inactivity in the left hemisphere, where many of the functions related to language are often processed. Another MRI taken some weeks after I'd left hospital showed that some of that inactivity remained, but that new activity had been registered nearby, and in the right hemisphere also. These MRI scans showed the old and new maps of how my brain got from thought to speech, and to the page.

When I saw that incredible MRI comparison, it barely registered with me. After the stroke, I desperately wanted to slip back into the grooves of my old life and by the time I was shown these MRIs, at a follow-up appointment at an office adjacent to the hospital, I had. The appointment was wedged between a gym session and film screening that day and, if there was no bad news, I just wanted to keep my day going.

I didn't want my brain to be medicalised. I didn't want to be thinking about the processes of internal combustion; I just wanted to be speeding on the open road.

The truth of the matter is that the neurological snapbacks like mine, so noticeable they can even be seen in an MRI, are both amazing and yet also a commonplace process that happens to every person in every moment of every day.

It may not be noticeable using current imaging technology, but everything we do changes us due to the processes of neuroplasticity. Every song we listen to, every conversation we have, every book we read, every emotion we feel, every moment of wonder we experience changes our brains. Even if we do exactly what we did the day before, we are changed as the neuronal processes used for that day are strengthened and further embedded, whether it be riding a bike, dancing the tango, loving your partner or praying to your god.

Thanks to neuroplasticity, we are what we do and where we are. The effects of neuroplasticity become a living history of ourselves. It underlies our thoughts and our future.

It's an unconscious driving force in the mind, working in tandem with another essential driving force, which can be unconscious, but can act consciously also. This other force can sometimes be engaged by choice and it can be engaged against our will. It, too, changes us, making us kinder or crueller, more efficient, more useful, more productive or less. It can reassure and calm us or it can drive us to the limits of insanity with clutter or intrusion.

This other driving force is memory.

Chapter 4

memory, childhood

I was the first of two Mckelvey kids to arrive. Born in Canberra Hospital on a crisp late winter morning in August 1976, I was taken to a tiny cottage in what was then bushland and is now the suburb of Harrison.

When I was born, my mum, Valerie, was on leave from her work as a primary school teacher and my dad, Valentine, was then working as the ACT administrator for the Australian Council, the federal arts funding body.

I don't think I have accessible memories from this period even though I can see the farmhouse, and the bush surroundings, and Mum and Dad, barefoot and looking four-fifths of the way towards being hippies. I think those memories may just be photographs that I've built stories around.

Before and after I was born, Dad brought a successful series of plays from Sydney, Melbourne and England to a city that was yet to have much theatre history. I have no memory of these plays.

Dad also helped conceive and launch the now legendary Canberra event called Sunday in the Park, in which tens of thousands of Canberrans visit Commonwealth Park to see theatre, hear music and participate in arts and crafts for free. This I do remember.

I was perhaps only three or four when Mum took me to Sunday in the Park, but I can see fragments of the event – images, feelings and snatches of noise. I can see people filing over a footbridge towards the sound of warbling trumpets. I can feel my hand in another hand.

With both of my parents born and raised in England, we had no family around and when my sister Laura came four years after I did, we were it: the Australian Mckelveys. We moved out of the bush, away from the snakes that Mum hated, and into suburbia, a ten-minute drive away.

Although I think my mum was sometimes overwhelmed by us two kids, my parents seemed generally happy then, in the bush village atmosphere of Canberra, in work they liked, and surrounded by a group of friends, most of whom were people Dad worked with.

I have only vague memories of these early suburban years. I remember snatches of houses we lived in, trips to see Mum's family, birthdays, family friends and a potpourri of nameless landscapes, experiences and people.

I started to really form memories in my first years in primary school, which was also when Dad left the Australia Council and started work at the Australian National University, becoming the general manager of the university theatre.

This theatre is a place I remember better than any home or even my school. When Dad took over, it had solid bones but neglected flesh. The stage, pit, wings, backstage, workshop, rehearsal and dressing rooms were all excellent for a 400-seat theatre, but the location and décor was unappealing. Theatre-goers were invited to a corner of the university that was dark and quiet at night, loitering in a long, unappointed cavern, before being called to uncomfortable, sticky vinyl bench seats.

Dad and a group of his friends managed to convert the utilitarian theatre into a place of baroque culture, where Canberra's elite donned tuxedos for a series of expensive performances, starting with a production of Handel's *Belshazzar*.

I don't really remember that production, but I remember the purple and gold paint, and the light fittings built in the workshop to look like candle-lit chandeliers, and the excitement. I remember it as a grand project and a success.

They used the money from the success of *Belshazzar* as the launching pad from which they revitalised and refurbished the entire theatre.

This refurbished theatre is the place where so many of my strongest childhood memories were captured. Forty years later, I can still see them and feel them.

I can feel the excitement as I arrive at the theatre on my BMX. I can see the loading door opening up to the workshop. I can hear the music playing on a tinny radio, see a set in the early stages of construction and I can smell the sawdust.

Dad is working but he stops when he sees me. He wipes his sweaty hands on his jeans and smiles as he walks towards me, bruises under a fingernail and flecks of paint on his neck.

I can see the foyer, too, abuzz with people. I'm in the little concession stand at the back, serving chocolates, chips and whiskey. I feel Dad's hand on the top of my head, and hear him asking me to collect glasses, or even tickets on the nights the theatre is shy an usher. I can remember the sound of a hundred adult conversations extinguished as I pressed the button activating the buzzer that urged people to take their seats.

I remember the shows best and am still able to recite lines or sing songs from them, from *Joseph and the Amazing Technicolour Dreamcoat*, a musical cast exclusively of Canberra buskers; *Equus*, a psycho-sexual drama; Molière's *The Misanthrope*; *Camelot*; and my dad's own production of *Man of La Mancha*, a musical treatment of Miguel de Cervantes' epic novel.

During these shows, I disappeared from the real world into another world. A more manageable and preferable world. That transportation happened in the theatre, but also in front of a television, or behind a book and later while holding a video-game console.

I wasn't running away from home, school or family – I was a generally happy child. I was just running to something that had more structure, order, sense and excitement than the difficulty, austerity, complication and boredom of the real world.

As a child, I was obsessively interested in stories and became frustrated when forced to engage in life's activities that I'd rather ignore. I didn't want to engage with the world as it was, but as it suited me. It was only when I was much older that I realised this was a trait I had inherited from my dad.

When I was a boy, I didn't investigate my dad, I just enjoyed him. He was gregarious and sometimes full of absurd whimsy. He was intelligent, passionate, intense and fun.

I never recognised that some people considered him a difficult person. I didn't see his tendency to be unyielding and his need to dominate conversation. I never thought about the fact that we didn't meet most of Dad's family, nor ever talk about them.

None of this was strange to me because, as children, we accept the reality that's presented to us. Mum was just Mum and Dad was just Dad. We didn't talk about Dad's family, even though we travelled across the world to see Mum's family. Dad could be expected to be at the theatre day or night, and Mum had to be available at all times, responsible as she was for everything Dad didn't want to be responsible for. That's just how it was.

It was only much later that I thought about any of that. It was only much later that I recognised that my dad was a unique character, reflecting an unusual and difficult youth. It was only much later that I realised Dad tried to live his life as though he could pick and choose which experiences and memories would be part of him. It was only after my stroke that I discovered that's not how life works, in no small part because that's not how memory works.

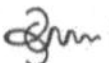

Science doesn't really understand the biological mechanism of how memory works, nor its evolutionary roots. It is believed that there are three distinct types of memory, known as procedural memory, semantic memory and episodic or autobiographical memory.

Procedural memory relates to skills and talents, like riding a bicycle or playing chess. Semantic memory relates to relatable basic knowledge, like knowing the names of the planets in the solar system or knowing which year the Battle of Marathon happened. Autobiographical memory is the sum of all the stories you tell about yourself to others and, most importantly, to yourself. Autobiographical is the type of memory that's most significant, to this book and to us all.

Autobiographical memory is the recollection of the day you met your spouse, or the moment you realised you wanted to become a lawyer. It's also the time you were assaulted, or did the assaulting. It's the moments in life that we desperately want to cherish and also the moments that we can't get away from. Autobiographical memory is essentially any experience you've had that, when asked about, you could tell a story about.

But what, of all the experiences of our lives, are chosen to be autobiographical memories and what experiences become experiential offcuts? This question is one of the scientific aspects of memory that's currently under investigation.

Some of the most impressive work in the field of memory being done is that of University of California neurobiologist and behavioural scientist Dr James McGaugh, who I interviewed for a podcast series I produced in 2020 called *A Theory of Mind.*

Dr McGaugh's work relates to the condition Highly Superior Autobiographical Memory or HSAM, a malady that Dr McGaugh discovered and named. Sufferers of HSAM experience an extreme surplus of autobiographical memory, like the first patient diagnosed with the condition, Jill Price, who approached Dr McGaugh in the late 1990s.

'What brought me to the doctors was the torment of my recall,' Price, now fifty-seven, once told a US radio station.

When tested, Dr McGaugh found that Price remembered almost every day of her life, recalling the weather on any given day, details of notable current events, or plotlines from television series that Price said she had watched. After McGaugh published his findings, Price became a minor celebrity and hundreds of people contacted Dr McGaugh claiming to have HSAM. A few dozen proved to have the condition.

In studying those patients, Dr McGaugh discovered two linked revelations about memory. The first was that brains have the capacity to retain and recall a huge amount of autobiographical memory in comparison to the amount that most of our brains do. The second was an abundance of memory was not a superpower, but a hindrance.

None of Dr McGaugh's subjects were particularly high achievers and most were tortured by the memories. Price, like many diagnosed with HSAM, was also diagnosed with depression. Dr McGaugh found that, without the selective nature of memory, his patients could not tell a coherent story of themselves. For the most part, the patients lived functional and fruitful lives, but also often sad lives.

For Price, the memory of her first kiss was just as clear in her mind as the slight drizzle that fell seventeen days after the third season of the TV show *ALF* began. Did the kiss and the drizzle mean the same thing to her? Price could say that the kiss was more important, but she didn't feel it.

An inability to place fog across all the inessential parts of life so that a path of memory could be carved towards meaning and purpose meant that Price's brain couldn't tell her the story of her own life.

For the rest of us, our brains *do* tell us the story of our lives.

I think often about the things I remember and those I have forgotten from around the time I suffered my stroke. My brain was damaged, my memory foggy. There are so many parties, concerts, conversations, events and moments that, in the wake of the stroke and my brain damage, I have no recollection of, even when prompted by friends or family.

There are, of course, other moments in that time that I remember vividly and which I've committed to text in this book, from memory, nearly twenty years later.

Why were some moments recorded and so many others completely discarded? I had no conscious hand in the decision. At the time, I wanted to deny that I was having a stroke, and then deny that it had changed me, and yet the things I strongly remember in that time almost all related to my stroke.

We still don't fully understand why or how our biographical memories are chosen, but it's acknowledged that emotion and memory are significantly linked. Joyful and remarkable events are often remembered, so too terrifying and desperate events.

If we are moulded by our memories, then we are moulded by our emotions. And we are very much moulded by our memories.

We are our emotions and our memories and the extent to which we can control or corral either is limited. We don't get to choose what's makes us sad or happy, and therefore we don't really get to control what becomes autobiographical memory.

What we get to control is how we react to our emotions and our memories. We also get to choose what we share.

Throughout my childhood, thoughts of my dad's own childhood and his young adulthood must have constantly been running through his mind, yet he never shared those thoughts with me.

Some fathers are full of stories about their lives, little gems and cautionary tales about morality and how the world worked. My dad had quips and diversions.

The thing about memory and emotion, though, is that it can't really be escaped. Even though they may refuse to be revealed in speech or text, memory and emotion often reveal themselves in behaviour, manner and mood. My dad never talked to me about his youth but, later in life, I think I understood it nonetheless.

Recently Dad left his autobiographical writing to me, and it was in those pages that I first discovered many of the details about his life and his family. While some of the detail was a surprise to me, none of the tenor was.

My grandmother was an Irish nationalist named Joan McEntee, born around the time of the Irish Civil War to Patrick and Mona McEntee, the owners and operators of a roving theatre fit-up company.

It was in the fit-up she met my grandfather, John Mckelvey, an English actor who had been denied entry into the British Army and was roaming Ireland looking for work.

Having shared stages with Gielgud, Guinness and Olivier, John Mckelvey was impressive to the fit-up company, and was impressive to Joan McEntee, who was wooed, married and taken to London after World War II.

In London, Joan and John had three children in quick succession: Louis, Valentine (my father) and then Siobhan.

Dad's writing left no inkling of what his early family life was like in London but I imagine it was a threadbare existence.

At age six, Dad and Louis were shipped off to the Silverlands Actor's Orphanage, a run-down manor house serving as a boarding school for the children of actors who couldn't (or wouldn't, as Dad noted in his papers) care for their children.

Shortly after the boys were deposited at Silverlands, Joan and John divorced and neither parent visited the boys regularly. Joan moved back to Ireland, taking baby Siobhan with her. John worked on England's post-war stages. Joan eventually returned to England, and then placed her daughter in the care of Silverlands also.

Silverlands would have been an interesting place to visit for a few days but for the children who were abandoned there, the hours, days, months and years would have been long. Dad spent six tender years in the orphanage and in that time he saw his mother only a few times. Dad wrote that his mother had developed a 'serious Irish thirst'.

Dad wrote fondly of Silverlands, and especially of Richard Attenborough, who ran the school, but I have often wondered about the dark secrets that may have been born among the abandoned children and the long, dark halls and bedchambers.

After the orphanage ran out of money and closed, the three Mckelvey children were deposited back with Joan and her new, much younger, husband Colin. Dad and Louis were sent off to a boarding school, this time a Catholic school run by nuns and priests, who were described by Dad as: 'narrow-minded, self-righteous, joyless, brutal individuals: living betrayals of all the fine principles they espoused'. There was violence at that school, with nuns and priests meting out discipline at the end of a cane or fist. There was also violence at the home the boys visited on holidays, with Joan and Colin often brawling verbally and physically.

By thirteen, Dad was running with a little gang of boys from the school, three of whom he became life-long friends with. One of them, Steve Morgan, a long, lanky boy who spoke in a slow drawl, became more of a brother to Dad than his own brother Louis.

Dad and Steve encouraged each other to leave school at fourteen. Steve entered the merchant marines while Dad stayed in London and started working at the Wimbledon Theatre, alongside his father who was a resident director. Dad fell in love with the theatre but he never seriously aspired to follow his parents' acting path, and instead seemed content working backstage, painting, sweeping and serving.

After two years, Steve arrived back in London with tattoos and stories about strange ports and strange people. Dad envied Steve's stories and experiences. There was a campaign at the time inviting British youth to populate the under-populated colony of Australia. Young men, in particular, were invited to relocate for free as part of the 'Big Brother Program'. With no prospect of adventure in England, the pair thought an ocean voyage across the world may suffice.

Dad and Steve had a year-long Australian adventure, roaming up and down the east coast, working here and there. Then Steve dropped an anvil on Dad. He was going to use all of his savings to go back to see his girlfriend in London. I know that must have broken Dad's heart.

Dad stayed in Australia, trying to save the money for a return passage to England. In June 1966, having developed a dangerous drinking habit, Dad decided to stow away on the *Patris*, a ship heading to Greece via Perth. He secreted himself in a toilet and waited as the *Patris* left dock. Dad's plan was to give himself up, but only after the ship was well free of Western Australia and on its way to Europe. His expectation was that he would be gaoled in Athens, where he assumed he'd be repatriated to England.

For a week or so, Dad slept in a janitor's room or a bathroom and ate only at the restaurant at breakfast time, when seating was unassigned. The rest of the time he sustained himself on the complimentary nuts and pretzels laid out in the bar. Then one morning, with the Western Australian coast in sight, guests were asked to assume assigned seats at breakfast.

The jig was up. Dad spent a month encased in Fremantle Gaol's old limestone walls.

When I recently read about Dad's prison stint, which coincided with his twentieth birthday, there were two things that I found hard to stomach. The first was Dad's inability to write at all about the feelings of fear, despair and longing I know he would have felt in prison. Instead he wrote jauntily and with diversion.

The second thing that was difficult to read was that, after being released from prison, Dad walked out of the prison's imposing gatehouse, down the street and saw a newspaper headline reading: 'ENGLAND WINS THE WORLD CUP'.

England winning the 1966 World Cup in his home country against the hated Germans was something Dad mentioned at least monthly, if not weekly, when I was a boy. That win was shorthand for all the happiness in the world, all accomplishment and joy. 'I've not felt that good since …' he'd say, or 'Yes, great, but it's not like …' and so on.

I'd always had a picture in my mind of what the final must have looked like for Dad. I saw row houses on an empty street, and tinny commentary coming from open windows. I saw an eruption of English cheers at each goal and mania when, as the final whistle blew, England were up over Germany 4–2.

I saw Dad and Steve literally dancing in the streets, with beer froth dripping from Dad's moustache.

But Dad hadn't been in England; he hadn't been with Steve; and he didn't even know of England's triumph until, alone and penniless and stranded on the edge of a lonely, parched continent, he read about it.

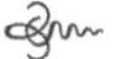

In 2017, I went back to Canberra to conduct some interviews and stopped in at Dad's theatre after hearing that it was scheduled for demolition.

The theatre was smaller than I remembered but, as I walked through the doors, there was a rush of feeling and recollection. I walked into the auditorium and interrupted an earnest teenager rehearsing something. I apologised and left. As I drove away, I called Dad, who was now living in Western Australia, to tell him that I'd visited the theatre on the eve of its destruction. I reported that the bar and café he'd built in his later years was not only still there, but humming, and the restaurant he'd opened, Vivaldi, was there also, operating successfully as Teatro Vivaldi, its own theatre–restaurant.

Dad seemed to be vaguely aware of the imminent demolition of the theatre. I had questions about the theatre and that time, but Dad didn't want to go down memory lane with me. He rarely wanted to reminisce, but this time I really wanted to share with him. I was flush with both emotion and memory, because I'd been at the theatre and because Dad had recently been diagnosed with cancer.

I didn't press him. I was older and, as best I could, I met Dad where he was then, and had stopped needing to try to figure him out to appreciate him. Dad had always been there for me, even though I recognised now his instinct may often have been not to be there. Some of his life was still a mystery to me, but that's okay. An enigma or not, I loved him.

Chapter 5

vertigo

I hated school. Primary school was okay, but the four years between year seven and ten were often grim.

Before I started high school, I took an aptitude test and was identified as a potential high achiever but, as I careened from one disastrous term to another, eventually to remedial classes, it became obvious that any potential I had was never going to be realised. This was something that left my parents frustrated (mostly Mum) and angry (mostly Dad).

I think a lot of my parents' frustration came from the fact I loved to learn and loved to read. But those loves existed in a narrow bandwidth. I first loved to read about the exciting and fantastical, moving from *The Faraway Tree* to *The Narnia Chronicles*, *The Lord of the Rings* and *The Once and Future King*, with a sprinkling of science fiction from authors like John Christopher and Orson Scott Card.

This led to books that were exciting and plausible, from *The Eagle of the Ninth* and Biggles books to Robin Cook, Michael Crichton and then Tom Clancy. I deeply loved Tom Clancy books, but Dad often mocked my obsession with them. I'd tell him about their plots and he'd scoff about their implausibility. Whenever I talked about Jack Ryan, the academic cum CIA analyst cum field operative at the centre of many of Clancy's books, Dad would interject and ask if I was talking about the 'super-genius violin and karate expert Jack Ryan? That Jack Ryan?'

Yes, Dad, that Jack Ryan.

Dad dared me to start reading his books, about the world wars, the Middle East, and his particular favourite, the activities of Mossad, which I did, enjoying greatly *Exodus* by Leon Uris and *Vengeance* by George Jonas.

I often had a book of my choosing in my school bag in place of some textbook I was supposed to have brought. In these books, I found a place that wasn't interminably boring.

Term after term, I brought awful report cards home. Dad and I fought. He didn't understand why I didn't do the classwork assigned in class. I didn't understand it either and yet the shame and frustration and detention that came from my laziness was easier to deal with than sitting down and applying myself. It's hard to explain even now.

I wanted to engage with the world and so many of the subjects I was failing – history, social sciences, physics – were topics I was actually intrigued about, but I just couldn't get into the groove of the way I was being taught. School was excruciatingly dull. I wished it wasn't, I tried to pretend it wasn't, but it was.

'Disruptive' was an often-used adjective in my school reports, and 'disinterested'.

It was only as an adult that I discovered that my mum believed I might have shared some behaviour and characteristics with the children she taught who were on the autism spectrum.

It's common now for adults to afford themselves some diagnosis of neurodevelopmental disorder or assign themselves as neurodiverse. I wouldn't deny anyone a self-diagnosis that helps them reconcile the past with the present, but I don't think I could be diagnosed as neurodiverse. A diagnosis of attention deficit hyperactivity disorder may have been appropriate, but I was a few years too early for that.

I do now allow myself the relief that, in high school, my mind was just irreconciled with my environment. Not every bad relationship has a villain and high school and I just weren't a match.

Back then, I didn't allow myself that relief. High school was a bedrock institution in my life, and when people and institutions are at odds, surely it could only be the fault of the individual.

High school was made bearable by two things: volleyball and my friends. For some reason, volleyball emerged as a popular sport in my class. I loved it (and still do) and when I showed some aptitude, I dedicated myself to it, as did some of my close friends.

We did quite well in inter-school competitions, even getting a little smattering of spectators when we played and, alongside two of the other kids in the school team, I was picked for the state team that competed in the national championships.

My volleyball friends were similarly at odds with school, and while volleyball was one of the ways we'd blanch the boredom of our high school experience, it wasn't the only one.

Some kids and parents considered us bad kids. We were all doing badly in school. We listened to NWA and Slayer. We got in fist fights and even had run-ins with the police, once spray painting a huge mural on the wall of a rival school when we were going through a hip-hop and graffiti stage, and once ending up in a seriously exhilarating but shockingly irresponsible 3 am car chase with police through Canberra's misty, cold, empty streets.

Trips to the police station and sombre calls from disappointed teachers certainly didn't improve my rocky relationship with Dad in my teenage years.

Thanks to volleyball, we weren't drinkers, drug takers or smokers, but we had the other hallmarks of being 'bad kids'. I sometimes found it hard to reconcile with that tag, but I had to admit that it fit. I enjoyed the wildness of my friends and I was careening towards an uncertain future.

It was at high school when I first felt the cold touch of depression and mania, following thoughts first introduced while in primary school.

'How are we doing against the enemy?' Dad asked me once as I sat on the bench seat of his yellow VW Kombi van. This was some time in the late 1980s. We were in the Canberra suburb of Fyshwick and it was a Saturday morning, warm, but only under the sun. I remember that. I remember lumber in the back of the van too, and the truckies café breakfast we'd just had.

'The enemy?' I asked Dad.

'Time,' he said. 'Time is always the enemy.'

I never forgot those words and the ice that rushed into my veins afterwards. Time *is* always the enemy.

Later, that thought came to me, with ominous and cold intent. It mostly came at night, as it still mostly does when it comes now. It manifests itself then as a suggestion that life is meaningless and perhaps even worthless.

I think my depression and mania and my schooling woes and propensity for wild behaviour were linked, but I don't think there was a cause-and-effect relationship. The relationship was more complex than that. It's possible that both my behaviour and my depression fuelled each other. It's also possible that they were both symptoms of some large, hidden complication or perhaps even an unusual neural morphology.

Either way, both drove a tendency for cynicism and a mild nihilism that sometimes spurred me to look at my future and say: 'If it burns, it burns.'

In 1993, I did find some educational relief. In the Canberra public school system, students are moved from their high school after the end of year ten to colleges where they are prepared for either university or the workplace. I moved to Dickson College, and there I finally found a learning environment that suited me. At Dickson, we assigned our own classes and our own hours and interacted with teachers as equals. At Dickson, I enjoyed the first decent report card of my post-primary school academic career.

At this time, one of Dad's closest friends had taken work running the Perth Theatre Trust and he asked Dad to move west to run His Majesty's Theatre, a genuine Edwardian building wrapped around a beautiful 1300-seat auditorium.

Mum didn't want to move to Perth. She'd just spearheaded an industrial action to protect individualised care and teaching at the Hartley Street Annex, the assisted learning centre integrating handicapped children into the adjacent primary school. This had resulted in the ACT education board handing over management of the annex to her. My sister, Laura, didn't want to move. She was just about to start high school with a large group of friends. I didn't want to move either as school was finally making sense to me.

The vote was 3–1 to stay, and yet we were going anyway.

It took a little while, but both Laura and I ended up loving Perth. I developed a deep affection for the place where we spent our first weeks as Western Australians. While we looked for a house to rent near the Perth Theatre Trust, we were put up in a holiday apartment across the road from Cottesloe Beach.

From the windows came the smell of fish and chips; from the balcony could be seen Norfolk pines, yellow sand and a shimmering, sapphire sea. It was late summer and yet it was gloriously hot. Cottesloe Beach was wonderful day and night, but it was at dusk that it became a place that beggared belief.

Sunsets in Cottesloe were an explosion of colour and peace. This was beauty like I'd never seen before. After we moved, I continued to gravitate to that beach. Eventually it became a place that was everything to me. I continued to play indoor volleyball in Perth, but not with the regularity that I played beach volleyball at Cottesloe.

In beach volleyball, I found a wonderful group of friends, varying in age, race, circumstance and non-volleyball interests. We spent so much time together, bathing ourselves in sun, salt and the endorphins of exercise.

Cottesloe became a place where my mind slowed down. We played games on the court, we sat on the hill talking about lives and became awed together when the sun set. Beach volleyball was, and continues to be, one of the healthiest and most positive aspects of my life.

For a while, I was quite good at beach volleyball. I wasn't explosive like some of the best players around me, but I had endurance and fitness and I always wanted to train. In 1996, I won the Western Australian under-18 beach volleyball championships with my close friend Geoff Goddard, who then won the Australian under-18 with me at Sydney's Manly Beach.

We followed that success with a Western Australian Institute of Sport scholarship and some middling results on Australia's national beach volleyball tour.

I was good, but never great. There was never any danger of me playing on the World Tour, on the AVP tour in the United States nor at the Olympics, as some of my friends had the capacity to do. But that has been a boon in my life because it's allowed me to play beach volleyball for my entire life, with only intermittent moments in which I've played the game with too much purpose and intent.

Instead the game has been a way to stay fit, a meditation, a social lubricant and, of course, a reason to spend a lot of time at the beaches close to the places I've ended up living.

After we moved to Perth, I had a brief stint as a student at Hollywood High School in the city's west. There I returned to my terrible student self, but found some great friends, who were less about fist fighting and car stealing and more about beer drinking and endlessly re-watching Quentin Tarantino films.

I was a sometime attendant of school in year eleven and then dropped out of high school in year twelve after a close friend in the Tarantino group, Rob, felt ill one day when he and I were out riding bikes when we were meant to be in class. He was diagnosed with a leukaemia that he was expected to survive but didn't.

Rob's cancer and my dropping out of school was coincidental, not causal, but it did mean I could be with him often, watching movies and playing video games. Sometimes we walked to the nearby basketball courts. Often we talked about small things and sometimes big things, although to try to talk about and understand the enormity of Rob's circumstance terrified me.

Rob lived with cancer for under a year. Sometimes he seemed well and sometimes he seemed sick and at times very sick. One day, he told me and two friends I usually visited him with that he had been told he had two weeks to live. We spent those weeks watching movies. Rob had been told that *Philadelphia* was good and we watched it with a couple of other friends, grimly realising what a terrible choice it was but not having the emotional wisdom to turn it off.

Rob died a few days afterwards. A call had come to the house while I was out and it fell to Dad to tell me what had happened.

I was devastated. The sadness was profound. I couldn't stop thinking about all that Rob would never experience. He had never had sex, never fallen in love, never travelled anywhere except Singapore. He was never going to hear Wu-Tang Clan's second album. He was never going to see those new *Star Wars* movies that George Lucas had announced.

I tried to deal with my feelings by just keeping things moving after Rob's death, scared of the minor depressions and manias I'd experienced in Canberra metastasising into something unmanageable. I managed it pretty well during the day and on weekends, staying busy with friends, volleyball and alcohol, something I'd just started embracing and was overindulging in regularly.

Sometimes I didn't manage it well. Sometimes, often at night, often Sunday nights, a cold hand reached into me and malignant whispers spoke to me.

'Rob was here and now he is gone. You are here and what next?' I would hear.

I'd try to think that voice away, thinking of all the good in my life. Usually it worked but sometimes it didn't.

When it didn't work, those dark thoughts spiralled. My life would get smaller and smaller, the universe larger and larger until I couldn't stand it any more.

The first time I bolted up out of bed and onto the empty night street in a panic was after Rob's death. It wasn't the last. In the wake of Rob's death, I always manage to calm myself after a late-night manic episode, thinking of all the good things in my future, all the fun and adventure that life offered then and would offer in years to come.

I didn't know that those manias were just precursive tremors.

I enrolled at a college that was more like Dickson and would allow me to take on the Tertiary Entrance Exams (TEE) as a private candidate. I did well on that test, recording a score in the nineties, meaning I could go to university and study pretty much anything I wanted except medicine and law.

This result was a shock to me and a bigger shock to Mum. I hadn't thought much about university in high school and chose a Bachelor of English majoring in journalism and minoring in creative writing, solely because the day my university preferences were due I watched the movie *The Killing Fields*, about an American and a Khmer journalist as the Khmer Rouge came to power in Cambodia. I was moved by the film and wondered whether I may be able to be a journalist. After watching the film, I also told myself I'd start saving so I could travel to Cambodia.

I enjoyed university. I had some incredible tutors whose extra-academic experience I greatly respected, especially Elizabeth Jolley, a wonderfully wise but unsentimental Western Australian literary great who taught me a lot about the nature of story.

I managed decent grades but I could never quite get over the feeling that I was a fraud. I'd never before been someone who voiced earnest and passionate opinions in class, never been someone who bared their feelings to contemporaries in my work. When I did those things, it sometimes felt like I was out of my own body, but it felt good also.

All in all, I grew a lot in that period. It was a wonderful time thanks, in no small part, to falling deeply in love with a tall, goofy, smart and altogether wonderful fellow English student named Kate.

I'd never shared thoughts with anyone like I did with Kate, and we connected, body and mind. I worked at a very fun bar and live music venue in the CBD. I played volleyball in the sun every weekend. Every book by Gabriel García

Márquez, Milan Kundera, Arthur C. Clarke, Ursula Le Guin, Hunter S. Thompson, Tom Wolfe or Isabel Allende was new to me. Life was undoubtedly excellent. Until it wasn't.

It started first again as intrusive thoughts and night mania, and then it became an all-day torture. One day, I woke up with the voice in my head and ice in my bloodstream. I bolted out of bed onto a daylit street and ran. I went back to bed and then bolted up again. This happened a few times. Eventually the mania left but a deep depression stayed. I was unable to budge the feeling that I was going through the pantomime of being alive while knowing that I was actually dead.

For two weeks, I was manic or depressed for every minute of the day. The smallness of life became microscopic; the vastness of time became everything. Existential vertigo was everywhere. This moment or another, it was all the same.

For the first week, I tried to keep moving, going to volleyball training and university and work. For the second week, I isolated myself as I didn't believe anyone could help me and I didn't want to infect anyone with what I believed was a terrible but undeniable truth about existence. I dodged my friends and family that week, and was especially reluctant to see Kate, knowing that she'd fought her own mental health battle in year eleven that saw her hospitalised for a while.

Eventually, one Saturday evening, Dad pressed me on what was going on. I know it was very hard for him to ask about my emotions, but it was even harder for him to see his son in pain. I explained, as best I could, how I felt. As I did, I was flushed with shame and embarrassment. Dad tried to help, bless him. He even talked to me about the relief of spiritual belief, something he didn't have.

Our discussion didn't help and the next day he asked me to go for a drive with him. I didn't ask where and he didn't tell me. We drove mostly in silence along Kings Park, down through the empty CBD and to the Royal Perth Adult Mental Health Inpatient Hospital. It was only later that I fully appreciated how Dad had taken me to get care, as at the time I was completely numb and able to communicate only with my own thoughts.

I spent a little more than a week in the hospital, mostly sitting on my bed alone. I sometimes talked to kind and well-meaning but ineffective counsellors, and sometimes attended group therapy with people who were not ruminating on existence but were deeply and structurally affected.

'I'm okay, but these people are crazy,' Billy Joel once said in an interview about his own time in a psychiatric hospital. It was one of the things that Dad used to say and something I thought of often while in hospital.

I refused drugs. I didn't think they applied to my situation, even though no other treatment seemed to work either.

One day, a professor of psychiatry was brought to my bed. He was grey-haired, bespectacled and taciturn.

'So, Ben, you can't enjoy your life?' he said.

'I think I enjoy it too much,' I told him.

I had thought it no coincidence that probably the happiest time in my young life was coinciding with a mental breakdown. I told him if life wasn't so good, I wouldn't worry so much that it would soon be over.

He was generous but direct in responding. 'Do you think you are the only person who has such thoughts? Everyone has such thoughts and, yet, look around you: there are people enjoying their lives.'

His eyes were firmly on me as his hand gently waved at people rocking backwards and forwards, people staring at walls from a short distance, people putting unlit cigarettes in and out of their mouths.

'Sartre had these thoughts, of course, but he enjoyed his life. He enjoyed conversation and wine.'

I didn't tell him, but I hadn't heard of Sartre.

'You're young. You don't know this yet but there is a

whole lifetime's worth of adventure just in the gradations of wine's subtle flavours. Do you drink wine?' he asked.

I told him I didn't.

'Do you have a sense of adventure?' he asked.

I told him I thought maybe I did. I didn't know yet.

'So, you have that. Hold on to it. You can have the whole world. You can have your adventures. You will be a different person because of them. You cannot pre-empt that.'

I thanked him, but didn't think anything he'd said had helped.

I went to bed on the ward that night thinking little of our conversation. To me, it felt like the meaningless and ephemeral nature of life was a core, fundamental truth and I didn't think that was something I'd forget just because there are a lot of different types of wine in the world.

But something had happened. I woke up renewed. I sat in the day's first rays of sun and was recharged. I enjoyed my grey eggs and my watery black tea. I enjoyed my surroundings, the music on the radio. I even enjoyed the *West Australian* newspaper.

I didn't want to investigate my improvement in case it disappeared under scrutiny, but I did anyway.

Had the simple suggestions that I fill my life with adventure changed my whole existential outlook? I didn't think so. Was it just that I was bored with depression, and that my brain had kicked out some neurochemical that quashed my fears? More likely.

I just felt good. Better. When I came home from hospital, Dad and I didn't talk about what had happened. We never talked about it. I just strode back into my life, leaving the past behind. Such was the Mckelvey way.

Kate and I reconnected and then decided to defer a semester of our studies and spend the time in Broome in northern Western Australia. I found a job teaching volleyball at a resort that both paid a wage and gave us accommodation, and Kate took on work as a waitress at another resort.

It was a magic time, with both of us completely lost in the beauty of the place and each other's company. We came back to Perth high on life. I went back to uni on the first day of semester, but Kate wasn't there.

Kate had suffered a relapse of her own a mental health issue and went into hospital.

I never understood exactly what was happening to her, but she told me that she felt like she was flying. I told her I thought that was a good thing, and she told me it usually was, but not now. I think she was suffering from her own experience of emotional vertigo. Despite my efforts to understand what was happening to her, I never really did.

Kate was adamant that she didn't want me to visit her in hospital, so I didn't.

I walked past her hospital often, slowly, hoping to see her in the window. I felt real, profound sadness, which was crushing and distinctly more bearable than what I'd felt during my stay in hospital.

Kate wasn't in hospital for days, like I had been, but months. She stopped texting and stopped calling and we lost contact completely.

I only ever saw Kate once more, when I returned to Perth in my late twenties. We allowed ourselves only a few minutes of 'what if' because we were then both old enough to know that 'what ifs' were just betting slips in the bin.

Dad left Mum at around the same time, leaving Laura and I too, I suppose. He didn't tell us that he was leaving, he just bought a campervan one day and drove away. I assumed he was having a holiday. Laura assumed that too. Only Mum knew what was happening.

Dad had just gone through a professional and personal crisis. He'd lost his job in a restructuring and had started an affair with a co-worker, Marlene.

When the days Dad had been gone for became weeks, Laura and I were becoming embarrassed and angry. I was even angry at my mum. I snapped at her one day, asking if Dad was ever coming back.

'You'll have to ask your father,' she snapped back.

I never did, because her response told me he wasn't. I was twenty-one then, roughly the age Dad had been when he decided he 'didn't have a family, but a familial catastrophe'. My sister was seventeen and Mum then just past fifty.

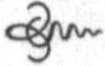

It was only later that I was outraged by how Dad's choices and callousness affected my mum. Perth wasn't Mum's home. Valerie Buggy's home had been Tunbridge Wells, where she lived in a respectable middle-class home with loving parents and sisters. Valerie Buggy's home had been Chester, the place where she was charmed by Dad, who was then on an upswing of respectability and working hard as a theatre house manager. Valerie McKelvey's home had been Liverpool, where Dad worked at the

Liverpool Playhouse and where Mum laid the foundations for her special education career, teaching in the infamous Liverpool 8 district.

Canberra became Mum's home also, a city she moved to via Melbourne after Dad told her, out of the blue, that he was returning to Australia and that she could come with him if she liked.

Mum didn't want to go. She'd just been made a deputy head at the school she was working at and she had family in England she loved, but she went and made it her home, with two Australian children born in Canberra and a tightknit group of friends earned.

Perth had been home, but now her husband had left her, her daughter was at an age when she wanted to finish school in Perth but not spend that much time with her mother, and her son was spending no time at home and was already planning his escape from the city she was stuck in to the east coast. That doesn't sound like home.

I'm embarrassed now how little I thought of my mum when Dad left, and how little I thought of my sister, when they needed my support the most. Like Dad, I sometimes had a selfish instinct to ignore and run away from my problems.

Chapter 6

a feast in the east

I got to Cambodia in 1999, where Khmer Rouge rebels were still being brought back in from the cold, guns and drugs were everywhere and some of the legendary Angkor Wat temples could be enjoyed by yourself.

The trip was about as much adventure as I could handle at the time, but it whet my appetite for more.

While in Cambodia, I was offered a job working at the Sydney Olympic Organising Committee and, after a quick visit back to Perth, I moved to Sydney.

I spent a few months writing athlete profiles for the official Olympic programs and then the editorial team I was part of moved to working on the Olympics.com website, where we prepared evergreen stories in preparation for the actual games.

When the Sydney Olympics started, I worked in the newsroom and went from venue to venue, gathering stories of major triumph and minor tragedy to upload. Every time I could, I went to Bondi Beach where the Olympic Beach Volleyball competition was being undertaken and that was pretty much a party every day, and every day my mind was blown with some experience or another.

A colour piece I wrote for the site allowed me to approach people who were attending the Olympics, like Chelsea Clinton, who gave great quotes, Muhammad Ali, who had little to say, and Bill Gates, who stared at me blankly before he gave a signal to his bodyguards, who dragged me away from him by the backpack.

It was surreal to see figures like this in the flesh, but frankly I was more in awe of the world-class volleyballers in attendance, especially the recently retired heroes of my youth who were now commentators, like Sinjin Smith, whose signature shorts I wore when I played, and Karch Kiraly, likely the best sand and court player volleyball ever had.

The undoubted highlight of the experience was, of course, the gold won by the Australian women's team of Natalie Cook and Kerri Pottharst, athletes I had trained with before the 1996 Atlanta games, and whose medal I wore that night as the small volleyball community drunkenly marked an unbelievable milestone at a nearby pub.

My love affair with the sands of Bondi Beach started during that tournament. It was a magic place I regularly came to play volleyball and swim afterwards, especially when the world became complicated or difficult.

After the cessation of the games, the excitement of the Sydney Olympics was replaced by the excitement of the city of Sydney itself.

After a stopgap job at a business-to-business newsletter, I was hired at *Juice*, a music and culture glossy magazine that was the main rival to *Rolling Stone*. My job was primarily interviewing musicians, singers and actors, reviewing albums, and commissioning and editing copy. And while ninety-five per cent of the job was office work, five per cent was the stuff of my early twenties' dreams.

In Australian music journalism, there seemed to be two types of writers. The first type were older and often jaded, but they knew a lot about the industry and the history of music and wrote very well about context and the technical aspects of composition and performing.

The second type were neophytes, who were less experienced writers but essential because the raw excitement of music appreciation permeated their copy and that meant they were often closer to the zeitgeist.

I was in the second group, and I think it was in part because I was in awe of the experiences I was having, and that I liked rap music and electronic dance music, that I ended up being promoted all the way to the editor's chair.

I cringe now thinking about how ill-informed many of my music reviews were, and thinking about the interviews I did with artists whose work I didn't understand at all. Despite this, there were a few stories that informed the type of work I'd do when I got my vocational shit together.

One such story was an assignment I took touring Timor-Leste with some Australian musicians who were doing little concerts at Australia's military bases in that country.

The story was designed to be a fly-on-the-wall experiential first-person story, with the bands at the centre of it. The *Almost Famous* assignment with flak jackets. When I got to Timor-Leste, I couldn't help become more interested in the locals, the soldiers, the mission and the Timor Gap Treaty, which regulates oil and gas exploration in the Timor Sea Seabed.

I saw how poor the Timorese were, and learned how significantly a new treaty that respected international norms would affect the country and its inhabitants. I learned how brutally the Australian government was behaving in their negotiations, fighting hard for a treaty that would be against international norms and would make no appreciable difference to Australian lives, except for those who had a financial interest in companies like Woodside and Rio Tinto.

I wrote about what I learned, and I also wrote about the Australian soldiers, who were mostly young men I liked and respected but who were also vehicles of policy, stated and unstated.

There were a few themes in that feature that would echo in books I wrote later about the activities of Australia's special forces in Afghanistan.

Another feature that had echoes of work I'd do later was a profile about Beyoncé Knowles, who at that time was attempting to break out of her group Destiny's Child and start a solo career. I met Beyoncé at Crown in Melbourne, then tagged along with her to Channel Ten Studios where I did an interview with her before she performed her first solo single.

We ended up having some real conversations and a real experience, which doesn't often happen when you're sent to profile someone as famous as she is.

Beyoncé was twenty years old then, seemingly with the world at her feet, but I could tell she didn't feel like that was the case. As soon as we met, she commented on my orange sneakers, which sparked a conversation about her new giant orange hairdo, which I loved but she was very nervous about.

'Not too much?' she asked.

Just the right amount, I thought.

I loved her new song too, which was 'Work it Out', written by my favourite producers The Neptunes. She wasn't sure about that song either. Perhaps it was too sparse, perhaps a bit too much of a throwback and perhaps not to be the hit that her bandmate Kelly Rowland's breakout single 'Dilemma' was.

Beyoncé struck me as someone who needed a holiday, and when I said as much, she was animated. She desperately wanted a holiday, something she hadn't enjoyed since the single 'No, No, No' came out when she was fifteen.

I asked her what her perfect holiday would be and she couldn't even imagine it.

She reached for: 'I guess a little house in Miami with a few girlfriends for a weekend?'

I laughed and asked her if that's the best she could come up with for her dream holiday.

When our time was up, she asked whether I needed

more time and of course I said I did. I watched her perform on *Rove Live*, we shared a lunch of Chiko Rolls and chocolate milk bought at the Channel Ten canteen, then she asked if I needed even more time, which I said I did, so we headed to the airport together with her little sister, Solange, tagging along.

It became pretty obvious some time that day that she just wanted to chat to someone, and that she was really only allowed to do that as work. Her whole life was work, and every minute an opportunity. This was the ethos driving Team Beyoncé, which, I realised pretty quickly, wasn't captained and coached by Beyoncé but her dad, Matthew Knowles. This was the man that the publicists, producers, bodyguards, stylists and drivers looked to when there was a question to be answered. This was the man Beyoncé looked to when she said that I needed more time.

That day, Beyoncé got some hours off from Matthew Knowles under the guise of work and I got one of the few features that I think I got right when working at *Juice*, because I managed to find a real connection with my interview subject, something that was relatively rare for me until I started writing books.

The day ended with myself and the Beyoncé entourage flying to Sydney, where we met up with the rest of Destiny's Child in preparation for their show at the Sydney

Entertainment Centre, and I met a friend for dumplings and beer and then the same show.

The last element needed for the story I wrote came in the first minute of the concert. I had been telling my friend about the quiet, melancholy girl I'd spent the day with when the lights dimmed, the crowd roared and the other Beyoncé appeared.

Flanked by her bandmates, Beyoncé waited for the roaring to abate and sang the first line of the song 'Independent Woman Part 1', asking the crowd to tell her what they thought about the star in front of them.

How did we feel? The roaring doubled, tripled then became a jet blast of approval. The beat dropped and Beyoncé (with help) slayed one of my favourite pop songs of the era. Destiny's Child were great, but Beyoncé was a rare superstar.

I yelled to my friend in the applause break that this Beyoncé was a whole other person. Yet she wasn't, and that's what made her and the story interesting.

Beyoncé was a nervous young woman, a domineered daughter, a style icon, virtuoso songwriter, a superstar performer and a thousand other things all at once.

When interviewing for profiles and biographies, the goal is often to create a space of trust where the subject feels comfortable showing many parts of themselves. When writing profiles or biographies, the goal is often to find links between those parts, creating a full and fascinating person of multitudes, and perhaps even contradictions, in the text.

I didn't know that then, of course. I was at the start of a writing journey of trial and error, and I was still a long way from believing I had any skills that could be utilised into writing I'd suggest anyone read.

When my stories were published, I never kept clippings of my work, never passed them on to friends and only ever spoke of my experiences at work, never the work itself.

I had my own multitudes. I was the editor of a magazine with a staff, a following, a budget and even a tiny little space in Australian music history, but I was still that kid who, deep down, was scared of all of the homework he was assigned.

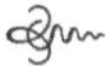

I just loved every day of those early years in Sydney. After some time in a true share house with sheets dividing the rooms instead of walls, I moved into an apartment above Porky's strip club in Kings Cross, smack bang in the middle of a city that was then radiating excitement. As I unearthed new groups of friends, scenes overlapped in glorious ways: the shimmering gay scene rippling out from Oxford Street, overlapping the club scene of the Cross and city, which I sometimes contributed to as a DJ. Then there was the grungy music scene, dotted through the east and inner west, the club scene, the after-work Aussie pub scene, the glamorous magazine scene, the arts scene, the serious media scene, the beach volleyball scene: there was always something to do in Sydney every day of the week. That's why I was out at a party when, one Monday night, the whole world changed and the trajectories of so many lives changed, including mine.

The first plane crashed into the World Trade Center at 10.46 pm on Monday, September 11, when I was sitting on the runway of an inner-city strip club.

I had been invited to the *Penthouse* magazine Pet of the Year Awards by a friend who worked at the company that published the magazine. The event was at a club called Minx Bar, which was one of a handful of 'reputable' strip clubs during the brief period in Sydney when it was relatively chic to attend this club or Dancers Cabaret in Kings Cross.

The first we heard about the attacks was when a girl in a blue wig, heels and a diving-V one-piece sat on the stage and explained to one of our friends what she'd just seen on a television backstage: a passenger plane smashing into one of the towers of the World Trade Center in New York. A friend and I left Minx in search of a television we could watch. We found four at a bar nearby, where tradies, alcoholics and gaming fiends were crouched over tap beer on stale carpets.

Only one television was showing the burning New York skyline, and no one in the bar had noticed the world was changing. My friend and I stared at the silent television as Creedence Clearwater Revival blasted from a nearby speaker. We watched United Airlines Flight 175 roar across the blue New York sky before becoming a ball of flame as it hit the World Trade Center tower. We yelled for the bartender to turn the music down and the television volume up.

They were strange hours, and then strange weeks, of rumour, fact and the *Drudge Report*. I read that dreck as I read everything else. Since I'd been the boy who migrated from Tom Clancy to George Jonas, I'd maintained an interest in national security and particularly in the geopolitics and history of the Middle East.

I already knew a little about Osama bin Laden and al-Qaeda even before 9/11. While US intelligence services didn't concentrate on bin Laden's organisation as they should have in the wake of the 1993 World Trade Center bombing, *Time* and *Newsweek*, magazines I had subscribed to in Perth and in Sydney, covered the organisation and the political and geographical context it existed in extensively.

I travelled through the United States a couple of months after 9/11 on a reporting trip and the airport was full of armed soldiers, as though al-Qaeda might arrive through an LAX terminal. The attack had been opportunistic and, frankly, an ingenious use of the limited resources al-Qaeda had then, but the massive loss of life and terribly spectacular nature of the attack had seemingly changed the basic principles of logic. Everyone in the United States, and even many in Australia, suffered a minor collective trauma on 9/11, and in the wake of that trauma it seemed reasonable to accept a surging American wave of militarism and patriotism, and geopolitical decision-making based on emotion.

Prime Minister John Howard committed Australian troops to the fight the day after the 9/11 attacks and when the American counter-attack on Afghanistan, where bin Laden and his group had planned the attacks, started in October 2001, the Australian Special Air Service were some of the first troops on the ground.

By March 2002, it seemed the war in Afghanistan was essentially over but the rage in the hearts of many

American people and in the White House was still running hot. At the same time, plans were already being finalised for an invasion of Iraq, which would be justified by what we would learn years later was false intelligence.

I knew a little bit about Iraq also, a country I had obsessed about during the 1991 Gulf War.

That war started when I was in Melbourne with my dad, having driven there in Dad's yellow Kombi van to see *The Phantom of the Opera.* We'd been in the menswear department of David Jones on Bourke Street, alongside about a dozen people, watching, on a small television above a rack of pants, Baghdad light up in plumes of yellow and white as F-117 stealth jets, B-2 bombers, F-series fighters and Tomahawk cruise missiles attacked the capital.

When we returned home to Canberra, I watched the rolling CNN coverage of the war, day and night, and read all that I could in the newspaper. I remember seeing a photograph of British bulldozers rolling over Iraqi positions and realising that all the Iraqi soldiers there must have been buried alive. Some of those men were only a few years older than me by then. I read that many of them were conscripts and clutching rifles with no ammunition.

I also remember watching news coverage of a coalition air attack against an Iraqi convoy on a packed highway leading out of Kuwait and later seeing images of the aftermath of the attack showing burning husks of military trucks, buses and cars, and charred litter that had once been hundreds of people.

I'd once had waking dreams as a boy of being Biggles or GI Joe on righteous missions of derring-do but after the Gulf War, I had military nightmares in which I was an Iraqi, waiting for a rumbling bulldozer or unseen bomb to violently end my life.

In February 2003, I went out onto the Sydney streets and protested with hundreds of thousands of other people, marching against the imminent invasion of Iraq.

I think most of those protesting shared the belief that a war against Iraq was unnecessary. The arguments being made by the Bush Administration and the Howard Government, that Iraq was somehow cooperating with al-Qaeda and developing weapons of mass destruction that may be handed over to a jihadi group like bin Laden's, seemed incomplete, confused or suspicious.

I was also protesting the unnecessary nature of the war, on behalf of the Iraqis who, if the conflict started, would suffer the fates my nightmares imagined.

I was also protesting for political domestic reasons. I hadn't been interested in politics as a kid nor as a young adult thanks, in no small part, because of the contempt

Dad had for politics and public servants and the antipathy he had even for elections, never voting himself. I felt strongly, however, that the Australian soldiers I'd met in Timor-Leste shouldn't be sent to fight in Iraq.

I had really liked most of the soldiers I'd met, and had been impressed by their professionalism and dedication to their jobs. I hated the idea of them being killed and maimed unnecessarily. I also hated the idea of them killing and maiming unnecessarily, using Australian shells and bullets firing from Australian tanks and guns. My first ever strongly held political position was that our country should not be involved in this war.

The Sydney protest was one of the largest in Australian history, and one of dozens of giant demonstrations across the world. They made no difference.

The Bush Administration wanted the Iraq War. The Howard Government was happy for the Iraq War to happen too. On 20 March 2003, Iraqis started dying under a massive American air bombardment. As the bombs landed, unbeknown to any of us, a secreted Australian Special Air Service Regiment contingent had already inserted into Iraq's western Iraqi desert.

As the Iraq War was being planned in Washington and Canberra, back in Sydney, the company that owned *Juice* magazine started to go out of business, first slowly and then very quickly. One day in December 2002, I was told to stop work on the issue I was working on. The next day, most people in the company were let go, but myself and the other editors and some art directors remained in the office as receivership assets.

We lingered in the office for a few weeks, sometimes meeting with those managing the receivership or people who were prospective purchasers of the company and its magazine assets. Then one day, I was told my job had been made redundant.

I was given a small severance cheque with another cheque promised should the receivers find the money for extravagances such as legally mandated redundancies.

Some who I worked with at that publishing company took the insolvency hard. Some were angry and some cried but I was strangely sanguine about the loss of a job that I'd thoroughly enjoyed.

I think my calm was due to a lack of confidence. The dissolution of the company felt perhaps even a blessing, happening as it did before I could be found out as a talentless charlatan.

By March 2003, I was looking for another job. While

some around me were already on their way towards having a 'career', I was just looking for a regular income and a way that I could keep the Sydney party going.

When I was offered a job at *Ralph* magazine, then Australia's biggest men's magazine, the role seemed to fit the bill.

The party certainly kept going at *Ralph*. I joined the magazine shortly after a new editor in chief, who set the standard that was expected of the staff as a heavy drinker who was barely ever in the office and wanted the magazine to be one part paean to sexual conquest and alcohol and one part anarchist's handbook.

The magazine was an environment that was as comfortable for me as I was unhealthy. In many ways, my own arrogance, cynicism and insecurity matched the culture around *Ralph* and I became increasingly misanthropic while threatening often to become a full-blown alcoholic.

I was happy, also. It was fun work and I did think there was virtue in the editorial. *Ralph* had been created as a response to the very nature of magazines, which was a steadfast dedication to subject matter that didn't really warrant dedication. *Ralph* was about everything and nothing. At its best, the magazine was absurd, sometimes even surreal, and if not anti-capitalistic, at least capital agnostic.

In 2023 meme language, a fashion magazine with the headline 'The biggest waste of time, talent and resources in the Australian media landscape' could be sitting next to a *Ralph* magazine with the headline 'Hold my beer'.

(Perhaps my favourite section in the magazine was 'Great Moments in History': two pages dedicated to a significant moment in the past, explained in the most absurd way possible. My favourite great moment detailed the Omaha Beach landing in 1944, laid out in hundreds of dollars of confectionary. A designer, a photographer and myself took a studio for a day so we could arrange Kit Kats, jelly babies, biscuits and mousse to look like Germans, Americans, landing craft and the defensive positions scarring the Normandy coast. At least a couple of days were dedicated to research and writing, because the page only worked if there was violence, detail and some sense of reality.)

When I started at *Ralph,* there was a strict demarcation between editorial and advertising, with the two staffs barely meeting initially. Editorial (which I was a part of) had a certain number of pages to create an environment that would bring in readers. The sales team could sell the other pages to Jack Daniel's or Holden or whatever. Then things changed. Some pages became co-owned by brands, with copy, imagery and ideas approved by advertisers.

Soon, even the purely editorial pages were co-owned. An interview I did with a filmmaker who ate only McDonald's for a month (and who became predictably ill afterwards) was binned due to fears that we may upset McDonald's, who may then tighten their advertising purse strings.

Ralph magazine slowly became less absurd and less representative of the people who worked there. That representation was one of the few weapons that magazines had in the face of the rising internet tide, as people might pay for a curated editorial experience, but not for a brochure.

The internet wasn't the only barbarian at the *Ralph* gate, either. A weekly men's magazine had been launched in Australia, which was flashier and trashier than any of the monthlies. When that magazine enjoyed healthy sales and captured a large slice of the advertising pie, *Ralph* started to emulate it, moving towards more suggestive shoots, shorter articles and lists passing as features, and humour that tended away from absurdism and towards retrograde sexism and racism.

I bitched and moaned in meetings about the editorial direction of the magazine, but to whatever extent I was right about the future, my complaints had nothing to do with any prescience and everything to do with the work I wanted to do personally.

The truth was, I gave less of a fuck about the magazine every month I worked on it. I'd become a lazy clock-watcher, overfed on booze, freebies and fun. I should have left *Ralph* before I had my stroke, but I didn't. I was in my mid-twenties: young, happy and healthy. I had fun at my job. Why would I leave?

Then I had my stroke. This should have been the moment in which I realised there was something better to do with my life than work at *The Footy Show: The Magazine*, but I had no epiphany. After the stroke, I just considered myself lucky that I worked in a place where there was no pressure to excel, or even turn in much work.

I was so relieved that life continued as it had before I'd had my stroke, and that the Sydney party rolled on, which is what I thought I wanted.

At the beginning of 2005, I had accrued a lot of leave and considered a big trip. I travelled quite often for work, often interstate and to the United States and Canada, and all of it was fun, but I really wanted an adventure.

At *Ralph*, we often did things that looked like adventure, but they were usually safe stage-managed PR exercises paid for by some advertiser or another. I wanted a real adventure. I wanted to see some of the world.

I'd just finished *The Great War for Civilisation*, the giant memoir of British journalist Robert Fisk that details his work covering the Middle Eastern conflicts preceding the 9/11 attacks. The detail, wonder and humanity of the book was vivid and enduring, and when I was told a few weeks later that I was going to be sent to the United States to cover a video game convention in LA, I decided to keep going and see some of the places Fisk had written about.

(I saw Robert Fisk once in Beirut, where he lived until his death in 2020. I stopped him and told him how much I loved his book and how it had affected me. He just stared at me blankly before saying 'Okay' and walking off.)

The trip ended up being thrilling even before I got to the Middle East. After finishing at the convention, I arranged to meet up with a well-known LAPD sheriff's deputy, 'Blondie', who was known for his anti-gang activities in the Los Angeles suburb of Compton. He asked me if I'd like to ride along with him on a shift in one of two Compton Gang Enforcement Team cars. It ended up being the one and (so far) only time I've been shot at.

The Compton Gang Enforcement Team was concerned with only one crime: murder. These cops weren't homicide detectives, who investigate killing, they were uniformed police who were as concerned with pre-empting killings as they were with finding those who had already killed.

Every shift, they spoke to informants, searched for weapons, executed warrants relating to guns and killings. Nearly every night, they were first on the scene when drive-by shootings happened, almost all of which happened between 9 pm and 11 pm.

The cops in my car drew their guns twice before we were shot at, once coming to the aid of other cops who stopped a gunpoint robbery and again when a suspect they wanted to talk to ran into a house and they feared he'd gone to get a gun.

We were shot at close to midnight, as the two cops I was with were all but apologising that it looked like I wasn't going to see the aftermath of a drive-by. Then the radio crackled. The other team was alerting us that they were pulling over a van that they believed had bullet holes in the rear.

It was a standard stop, not raising anyone's hackles until the radio crackled again and there was frantic shouting for help as the sound of automatic gunfire spat violence through a speaker.

We were only a couple of blocks away and, with screeching tyres and screaming sirens, we were there in seconds. The other cop car was peppered with bullet holes and there were casings from the Gang Enforcement Team sheriff's pistols scattered on the ground.

I jumped out of the car with Blondie and his partner when gunshots rang out in the dark street, cracking above and from where the other cops were trying to find the gunmen.

Blondie yelled at me to get the fuck back in the car and he ran off with his partner Tim into the night.

As I got back into the car, all I felt was exhilaration. Excitement. I finally had the perfect *Ralph* feature.

It was only later that I thought about the human tragedy of the night, when SWAT arrived and helicopters blasted loudspeakers telling people in family homes that officers were coming into their homes and that they and their children should lay on the floor with their hands on their heads.

And when Tim broke down crying, telling me that his thirty-five-year-old partner, Jerry, had been shot in the head and killed at a housing project in the nearby suburb of Hawaiian Gardens.

When they found the shooter, who looked like he was eighteen, it turned out he had shot at the deputies because he already had two felony charges and a third, possession of an unlicensed firearm, would put him afoul of California's three-strike rule and send him to prison for life. Why not try to shoot his way out?

Blondie told me he missed the 1980s when the gangs of Compton were killing each other with five times the frequency that they do now.

That story was the last I wrote on the staff of *Ralph* magazine, and was easily my best. It was funny and sad and certainly something some could enjoy on the shitter. It was a travelogue, however. Nothing more than a tourist guide to someone else's misery.

From LA, I flew to New York and then on to London where I met my sister, who was working on a ship on the Thames, and my mum, who was visiting her sisters. From London, the three of us flew to Italy.

As soon as we arrived in Italy, I received a message that the editor of *Ralph* was moving on and that a close friend was replacing him. I loved this guy and would have loved to have been in an office with him but, coming from a kids' magazine and promising a focus on integration, sexualisation and maximisation of profit, I didn't think he was going to be editing a *Ralph* magazine that I wanted to work on.

I was scared to leave the magazine, though. Since my stroke, I could write again, but slowly, and it felt like perhaps my tendency for the wandering interest and hyperactivity of my high school years had returned. That or I was just being a lazy shit because I could be. Either way, I was scared of what a post-*Ralph* future might look like.

I didn't share my feelings with my sister and Mum, though, as we weren't much of a sharing family. Until a few days later when I yelled it all at my sister in the middle of an argument we were having about some insignificant issue. She yelled at me also, finally telling me what was festering in her, which was the break-up of a boyfriend who later became her lovely husband and is now the father of my three nieces.

The yelling stopped when my mum started crying. She then shouted, asking why we couldn't be civil so she could enjoy her holiday.

Standing as we were in Italy, under the shade of Mount Vesuvius, on a long Roman road in Pompeii, with some of the most incredible ancient architecture around us and next to a mother we'd abandoned in Perth, her request seemed very reasonable.

Laura and I stopped arguing and we had a wonderful day, then a wonderful holiday, sharing thoughts, fears and feelings over pizza, pasta, wine and coffee in a way the three of us never really had before.

It was a lovely, gratifying and strengthening trip that was one reason the relationship between my mother, my sister and I changed. The other reason was the lightning that was to strike in a couple of months' time.

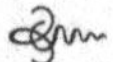

My Middle Eastern plan was to fly to Istanbul, get a visa for Syria then fly on to Gaziantep and, get a *servise* across the Syrian border, work my way south to Damascus, then overland to Jordan, on to Lebanon, drive back to Jordan and finally cross into Israel, where I'd eventually head home.

Even pre-war Syria had little travel infrastructure but the place was what I dreamed it to be: packed ancient souks, crusader castles, shimmering marble mosques and, everywhere, people with a story. Like most Arabs, the Syrians are terrifying enemies but superlative hosts.

As a guest in their country, Syrians consistently showered me with gifts, stories, cups of tea and meals. And one terrifying and exhilarating night.

In the old souk in Aleppo, under the shade of the one of the world's oldest and largest citadels, I saw a rare young Western man.

He was an American post-graduate student of Arabic named Cole who I befriended and one night, while drinking foul, cloudy beer at an unmarked tavern (drinking in a bar in Syria was then like attending an injecting room), he told me he was part of a university feeder program for an Other Government Agency, possibly a listening agency like the National Security Agency or perhaps the CIA.

After leaving the bar, we saw, through a large window, a football game on a television screen. A man named Suleyman beckoned us into what looked like an ornate office. We entered and so started a very long night.

Suleyman wanted drinking buddies. He gave us whiskey, which appeared on silver platters carried by one of two manservants. Suleyman showed off his large collection of guns, then said he was taking us to dinner, piling us into a large black Mercedes. He drove us through the night, into the desert. He was drinking whiskey straight and driving very fast. In a small town perhaps forty minutes from Aleppo, we were moved from one Mercedes to another, which was waiting with more whiskey. Suleyman drove us to the gate of one of Bashar al-Assad's secret prisons, just so we could see it, shaking his head mournfully, either at the inmates or the way they were being treated or both. Then we were back in the desert.

We rocketed though the night, with Cole and me drinking straight whiskey, so there was less for the increasingly wild Suleyman, and throwing furtive glances to each other when we could.

We were driving east and sometimes we saw signposts telling us that we were on the road to Tabqah, Raqqa and eventually Iraq.

I was intensely interested in Iraq then and read everything I could about it. The beheading of Westerners had just begun, so I didn't want to go there, especially as the guest of a drunken armed madman and seemingly in cahoots with an American baby spy.

Cole asked sometimes in Arabic where we were going and each time Suleyman told us we were going to a restaurant. His favourite restaurant.

Well after midnight, after almost two hours in the car, we arrived at the gate of a military airfield. We were waved inside and the car drove past MiG and Sukhoi fighters and bombers, and military helicopters and fighting vehicles before, to our great surprise and delight, we pulled up at a gorgeous little garden restaurant, full of Syrian government types and their guests.

By the time we sat down to eat, Suleyman was drunk and while the first courses of a meal of dips, falafel, kofta, spiced kebabs, pilaf, fattoush and tabouleh salad, mint tea and more whiskey were convivial, Suleyman became increasingly belligerent with every bite and every sip.

People stared as Suleyman ate and drank whiskey with Westerners. He asked us if we'd been to Paris, London or New York and bubbled with fury when we said we had. We tried to flatter him with compliments and ask about his life, but each question was met with another, slurred and angry.

Cole and I tried to keep things light, but when it became apparent he was suggesting I was an Israeli ('Binyamin … Binyamin …' he kept grunting at me), Cole said he needed to take a leak, beckoning me to come.

'We have to leave,' he said. I agreed, but how? Cole suggested the safest course of action for us was to thank our guest and simply try to walk out of the airbase and into the desert.

We did that and we were met with slurred abuse. Suleyman followed us. We kept thanking him. He performatively started calling people on his phone, telling them to meet him. We kept thanking him as we walked out of the restaurant and along the long road towards the airbase gate.

We were picked up by some Kurds in a minivan who worked in the restaurant. Suleyman's Mercedes followed the minivan for five minutes or so before driving off into the night. The Kurds dropped Cole and me off in a village nearby where we paid someone to take us back to Aleppo.

I arrived at my guesthouse at dawn and the woman who ran the place was waiting for me. I told her about my night and she said it would be safest for me and her if I packed my bags and left the city. I showered, drank some strong coffee and did just that.

I was happy to not risk seeing Suleyman again. The guesthouse owner's reaction, and Suleyman's actions that night, had shown me how dangerous he probably was. I also felt like I understood him. He was trapped, like most Syrians. Unlike many of his countrymen, he had money, but I think he was confined by his circumstance as an Assadist *apparatchik* and by the limited freedoms his passport afforded him.

After time in Hama and Homs, I went to maddening, hectic, hot, intermittently beautiful and always interesting Damascus then, on 12 July, I tried to enter Lebanon through the Masnaa Border Crossing, at the foot of one of the desert hills separating the two countries. I was denied entry. It wasn't just me, it was everyone: Syrian, Lebanese, Australian. It was only the next day that I found out why.

Hezbollah fighters had secreted themselves into Israel and attacked an Israeli military police outpost, reportedly in response to the Israel Defense Force's kill/capture program. Hezbollah had killed eight Israeli servicemen and captured two more. Retaliation was expected and the

Lebanese government, often at odds with Hezbollah itself, had closed the border in preparation for what may come next. What came next was full-blown war.

I took a *servise* taxi instead to Jordan and, after visiting Amman, Wadi Rum and Petra, I went to Allenby Crossing where, in principle, I would be able to cross into Israel. I was able to do so but, with a Syrian visa in my passport, only after a full day of waiting and watching Apache helicopters and fighter jets roar north into Lebanon then south back home.

In Jerusalem, Tel Aviv and even in the occupied territories, life was largely normal. Even in the north of Israel, where Hezbollah rockets sometimes landed, a friend of a friend invited me to a rave in a massive bomb shelter. It was in Israel, with only a few days before my return, that I realised that there was no way I could go back to my job at *Ralph*.

There was a world out there, of places but also emotions, stories and experiences and, knowing that, I couldn't return to that office and write another listicle sponsored by an alcohol company, or struggle my way through a sexually focused interview with a nineteen-year-old.

I wasn't confident that I'd be able to do more than what I was already doing at *Ralph*. I was still uncertain about my brain and my prospects outside the magazine. I was a slow writer, often listless and lazy, something I had attributed to my stroke.

The magazine was an unhealthy environment. I was a cynic when working there, like many of the people I worked with, and there was an inherent sexism in the work that permeated my attitudes also. I had become cloistered, however, especially after my stroke, and I feared what may be next from me.

In Israel, I figured it didn't matter what happened next. What mattered was just that I left. The worst that may happen is that I wouldn't find a magazine job and that I'd have to find an unskilled job until I figured out what to do next. That was the absolute worst that may happen, and that wasn't so bad. Working outside as a labourer must have its perks, and movie ushers seemed relatively happy.

As I flew back to Sydney from Tel Aviv, I even entertained the best-case scenarios. I ate modern military books up like M&Ms and was rarely seen without a book by someone like George Packer, David Finkel, Dexter Filkins or Mark Bowden under my arm. Maybe it wasn't too late to try to do something approximating what they did. Maybe I could go back to the Middle East and do some freelancing there, and maybe that work could convert into more work.

It felt like a pie in the sky dream, but isn't that what your twenties are for? Pie in the sky dreams?

Twelve or so hours after landing in Sydney, I was in the outgoing editor's office handing him an envelope in which there was a sheet of paper with one giant word on it: RESIGNATION.

He opened the letter and chuckled. I chuckled too.

'Right-o,' he said.

That was that. As per my contract, I would be unemployed in three months. What came next I had no idea, but I had some time to figure it out. I sent emails to as many editors of Australian magazines as I could, telling them that I would soon be available for freelance work. I also responded to a press release from the Australian Defence Force looking for expressions of interests from journalists who may want to spend time with Australian forces in the field. I thought my application a slightly baited hook into unlikely waters, but it was worth a try.

Then, a few days after handing in my resignation, a spasm of pain sharded from the top of my breastbone, left and right towards my shoulders and up at my throat. I clutched at my chest, sat down on a concrete planter and started to have a heart attack.

Chapter 7

a scar is also skin

I'd been on my way to join a group of my friends to attend an Asian Cup football qualifier between the Socceroos and Kuwait when it happened.

I was walking from the *Ralph* office to the spot where we all planned to meet, when I saw my friend Tom on a bus going by. I tried to run alongside Tom and the bus, which I did for a while before something grabbed at the top of my chest. I stopped and tried to stretch the pain away but no matter what I did there was a bony hand inside the top of my rib cage, grabbing at me.

The bus stopped and Tom got out. Two other friends appeared. I didn't say anything but was still stretching to ease the pain. Someone hailed a taxi. In the taxi, I was still gripped by the pain. I was silent, squirming uncomfortably while my friends chatted.

'Are you okay?' one friend asked.

It felt embarrassing to say that I had chest pains. I said it, though. There was an unusual quiet in the taxi after I spoke. I said I was fine. More quiet. After a minute, a friend suggested we go to the hospital, but I didn't want that. By the power of positive thinking, I was sure we could drive on to the stadium, the pain would abate and my life could continue as normal.

After a couple more quiet minutes, a friend asked if I was still feeling the pain and I admitted I was. We were about to pass St Vincent's Hospital and, when the pain became more acute, I agreed to stop.

I was being assessed at St Vincent's Hospital emergency. Again. By the time I saw a doctor, the pain had subsided. He asked about the pain and I told him it had been manageable. After he took a quick peek at my chart and saw the details of my stroke there, I was off to theatre.

An Irish surgeon conducted a nuclear cardiac test on me. This test involves a mildly radioactive dye being injected into your blood so it can be seen starkly against the rest of the body's tissue as the four chambers of the heart are checked for a blockage.

The surgeon, in scrubs and mask, chatted to me as he worked. I lay in a flimsy hospital gown on a surgical bed under blanching lights.

'Oh, it's a beautiful thing,' he sang to me of my first cardiac chamber, and similarly of the second chamber. 'Gorgeous, I'd hang a picture of this in my front room,' he said of the third chamber. Then he looked at the fourth chamber and, after a beat, said: 'Oh ... oh, no.'

I'd been lying, staring straight ahead at the ceiling and the surgeon swung an articulated monitor into my field of view. A cardiac chamber appeared on the screen. I could see a strong line of iridescence branching into an entire root system of light.

'This is a healthy chamber,' he said. 'And this ...' – he pressed some buttons – '... is not.'

I saw the same image as before, except without the root system of light. I saw a base of strong, iridescent light fading into darkness. He pressed his finger at the point of contrast.

'I'm sorry to say that this is your heart attack.'

I was shocked into silence.

'You're in the best place for it to happen,' he answered, rubbing my shoulder.

He told me he was going to put some stents – tiny metal coils – into my heart and asked if he could put some music on as he worked. He disappeared and the song 'Father and Son' by the artist then known as Cat Stevens came on over a sound system. It's a maudlin song about a man contemplating relationships at the end of his life.

I smiled for a moment knowing that, if I survived, I would one day find the situation and song very funny.

Then I cried as I tried to breathe my way back from the edge of another existential black hole. I waited for my mood to tip me over into a spiral of existential vertigo.

During my years in Sydney, I'd still had nights in which I was manic, and some days also. Lying in the hospital bed while I recovered, I thought for sure that voice and those choking hands would come back and, if they did, I feared they might kill me. I knew my heart was damaged and I didn't have faith that it could survive the deeply depressive weeks I'd had in Perth.

I spent the next ten days in hospital, waiting for the moment I fell into that vertigo again, and fearing it.

There were no moments of euphoria during that hospital stay, as there had been the last time I had been admitted. I saw no improvement nor any decline; I was just there, in hospital with a ticking time bomb in my chest.

After the surgeon put the stents into my heart, I was taken to a ward. Once again, as with my stroke, there was a period of investigation. The heart attack was evidence now of something more complicated. There must be a root cause. A reason why I'd had a stroke and now a heart attack. In a scan, a series of blood clots was found in my hip. For a few days, a nurse injected me with heparin, a strong haematological drug, and then afterwards I injected myself.

Again, the doctors found nothing specific in my blood that could be creating the clot that had wedged into my brain two years earlier and now perhaps in my heart. Something was happening in my body, and it was something that would kill me if it wasn't resolved. This time it may have been clots, next time it could be something else. The doctors speculated that it was perhaps related to the aortic valve in my heart, which had two cusps instead of the normal three.

This bicuspid valve was a congenital issue that had been diagnosed at my birth and had been monitored throughout my childhood. Back then, it was suggested that I'd likely have some cardiac deficiency but none emerged, and my cardiovascular fitness was very good throughout my teen years and twenties. Nothing suggested the valve was stenotic, meaning it was brittle and dangerous. Except that, at age twenty-nine, two years after my stroke, I had just had a heart attack.

There was a fear that perhaps the valve was stenotic, and that the atrophied area may have sent small particles of tissues into the heart or brain. How could that have related to the clots in my hip? It couldn't. It may have just been two things happening concurrently and independently.

A cadre of doctors, led by my cardiologist, decided on a course of action. I'd leave the hospital and continue with the heparin and, when I was well enough, I would go under the knife to replace the aortic valve in my heart. I was released a few weeks before my thirtieth birthday, which I spent at home, mostly asleep and under the influence of anti-depressants, prescribed to me after I had fallen into a deep depressive funk.

These were discontinued a few days after my birthday, as they were making me narcoleptic. A fear of my upcoming surgery soon wrapped itself around my bones and around my brain. I couldn't do any of the things I'd done in the past to shake the terror when vertiginous fear arose. I couldn't run. I couldn't play volleyball. I couldn't go out drinking with my friends. I couldn't make plans to travel. I was at home, waiting, waiting, waiting and fearing, fearing, fearing.

My surgeon was Dr Phillip Spratt, Director of Heart and Lung Surgery Transplantation at St Vincent's

Hospital. He arrived on the ward a few days after my heart attack, exactly when I was told he would. This punctual occurrence was rare in hospital, but he was a laser through the hospital cloud, cutting through the chaos of comings and goings. The hospital arranged itself around Dr Spratt's schedule. He was the Greenwich Observatory.

Dr Spratt seemed exceptional at masking regular human frailties, like emotion. As this thin man looked at my charts and talked about the surgery, I was taken aback by his flatter-than-a-lake disposition. For me, what we were discussing was my life and death; for him, it was work.

Work that he excelled at, though. When Dr Spratt explained that he wished to personally conduct my surgery, even if I chose to be a public patient, I was very happy. He explained there was still the possibility of serious complications.

'Serious complications?' I asked.

'Yes, serious complications,' he said.

'Resulting in?'

'Death.'

He told me the percentage chance of a serious complication during the surgery. It wasn't high, but it wasn't low either. The surgery would be more dangerous than landing on Omaha Beach during the D-Day landings, but it wasn't more dangerous than being in the first wave;

more dangerous than launching in a space shuttle, but less dangerous than launching in a Gemini capsule. The likelihood of serious complications was the same likelihood of being dealt a good pocket pair when playing Texas Hold 'Em poker. And I had been dealt plenty of those.

I don't know whether it was the possibility of serious complications during surgery that I feared, or the abject lack of control that came with surgery, but I became obsessed about the point of time in which I'd go under anaesthetic.

I was going to be asleep for a decisive moment of life and death and that fact may have been what was affecting me so much. I hated the fact that I would willingly drive to the hospital, check myself in, walk to a surgery bed, breathe in the gas and then ... what?

I later thought of Tom Wolfe's book *The Right Stuff* about US test pilots and the Mercury space program that proceeded the Gemini space program. The book's title isn't referring to tangible qualities that existed in the pilots and astronauts who were then America's greatest heroes, but to an intangible and fictional quality perceived by the pilots and astronauts as the difference between life and death in vehicles that randomly exploded.

Wolfe explained that, after a death, surviving pilots had to tell themselves that they had The Right Stuff and the dead didn't. It was the only way they could keep going back up.

I was about to undertake the most dangerous activity of my life and the most crucial moments would happen while I was unconscious. I very much struggled with that fact and even asked my doctor whether open-heart surgery was ever done under local anaesthetic.

Later, when working with combat veterans, I learned how much the loss of perception of control can contribute to post-traumatic stress disorder (PTSD), and how a breakdown often comes when the indifference and chaos of existence cannot be denied.

My GP suggested hypnotherapy to cope with my mounting fear. Desperate to stop a slide that I feared might end in a dangerous vertiginous panic, I agreed to do it.

In my sessions, my therapist often described a beach and the sound of the waves as they tried to put me in a comfortable, relaxed and hopefully susceptible state, where suggestions may be embedded into my consciousness.

The therapist would often put me in hammock and describe the warmth in the air, the sound of the ocean and the feeling of contentedness, attempting to pry away any intruding memory of the therapy rooms, and the bus ride there, conversations had that morning or any of the clutter that sits in the RAM of our brains at any point in time.

Eventually my therapist attempted to access and insert an idea deep in my unconscious: the idea that I should be relaxed about my upcoming surgery and that I should generally stop fearing my cardiac issues.

I wasn't hopeful that the therapy would work. Studies have found that only a small percentage of the population is highly hypnotisable, perhaps just one in ten. As I listened to my therapist describe a safe and successful surgery, I thought of how conscious I was and how I was one of the nine.

When I left each session, I thanked my therapist while also thinking that nothing much had happened.

Yet I think something had. I had happy moments. I listened to The Beatles, I let sun fall on my face. I put my feet in the sand every day and swam in the ocean.

I was still scared of what might be coming, certainly, but the anchor of present joys kept me from drifting into despair.

Like the professor who visited me at the psychiatric hospital, perhaps hypnotherapy's light touch was all that I needed. Perhaps my mind just needed an excuse to stop worrying so much.

On the morning of my surgery, I admitted myself into hospital and, as I waited to be taken into theatre, I was visited by Dr Spratt who had a spring in his step and even a smile on his face. He left with an 'I'll see you down there.'

My anaesthetist came next, who I remember little about, and then my perfusionist, a specialist attending to the cardiopulmonary bypass pump or CBP, who I remember vividly. He arrived with a folder of laminated images and documents and a speech about the things he wanted me to know about the possibility of neurocognitive decline and emotional change in the wake of the surgery due to time on the CBP.

During open-heart surgery, the patient's heart must be stopped and dry, so all of the blood coming into the heart must be diverted into a machine, the CBP, which simulates the heart's process of oxygenation. At the end of the surgery, the heart is started again, the CBP diversions are undiverted and blood is again processed naturally through the heart.

Patients often suffer cognitive declines or emotional changes after heart surgery. Some of those changes are, it's assumed, due to micro-debris and tiny air bubbles being passed from the CBP into the brain, embedding in the folds of brain tissue and creating minor brain damage. Some are due to tiny, undetectable strokes that can occur during surgery, or to imperfect oxygen transportation. Some of those changes are assumed to be emotional also, with the patient having to reconcile with the violence of their surgery and the possibility of 'serious complications'.

These changes are called post-perfusion syndrome, or 'pump head'. While pump head usually can't be recognised in fMRI scanning, it shows up in cognitive and IQ testing, self-reported depression and in the divorce rate of patients, which is especially high after long open-heart surgeries.

There was nothing I could do about it. I was strapped in, on the launchpad. I was on a ward and I was waiting. I was sucking ice blocks as the time since I'd been able to drink water passed twenty hours. I stressed. I was given a sedative injection. I floated on my bed to pre-theatre. I floated to theatre.

I heard commonplace banter darting backwards and forwards over me in a lift. My chest was shaved. Dr Spratt arrived in surgical scrubs. A plastic mask was placed over my mouth and nose. I counted from ten to nine to eight to ...

I awoke with a tube down my throat that was doing my breathing and a large cage over my chest, protecting a cardiac wound I couldn't yet feel. The drugs were still soaring though me but I could feel delightful and delicious consciousness.

I drank it in deeply. It was quiet and dark in the recovery room, but not silent nor pitch black. I ate up the quiet hums and beeps, the shuffle of feet. I devoured the sight of other beds in my peripheral vision, illuminated by the soft green glow of the displays on medical machinery.

I could hear, I could see, I was on the other side. It felt incredible.

I drifted in and out of sleep and, once in the fringes, I sensed someone at my bed. They reached down to attend to my cardiac wound. As they pulled away, I came alive and my hand reached out for theirs. I caught it weakly.

'Hello. What do you need?' a voice whispered.

I pulled the figure towards me best I could.

The figure chuckled. 'You want a hug.'

Touch. Such a delight. I went out again and then remember awakening. From where I lay, I had a direct line of sight to the ICU entrance and when I rose I saw my mum's face, and my sister's, peering through a window in the door.

I didn't know that they were coming and I was overwhelmed to see them. Gratitude rushed through me. Gratitude and hope. I had a life ahead of me.

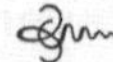

The first and second days after an open-heart surgery are intense, mostly because you are forced to your feet regularly to keep fluid from building up in your lungs. As you stand, it feels as though you've been torn in half and put back together again. There's a lot of pain in the first couple of days, and you know when someone new arrives on the ward by the grunting and yelling.

By the third day, you're up and walking. I got into the rhythm of a slow shuffle while listening to 'Kick, Push' by Lupe Fiasco and 'A Roller Skating Jam Named "Saturdays"' by De La Soul and, of course, 'California Love,' a song that reminded me of my stroke, but was also just an undeniable banger.

Each day, I put my headphones on and went up and down the ward, up and down. Each day, I became more confident in my stride.

Some days in hospital, I felt fairly emotionally robust. I was weak and in pain, but I felt that I was trending in the right direction, and sometimes that's all you need in life. I was ready to feel better and re-enter the world.

Sometimes I didn't feel like that. I felt exposed and as though my skin had been torn off. I felt I had no protection against any of life's attacks, minor or major.

Having my mum and sister in the hospital with me was calming. The dynamic between us had changed from what I'd known when we had all been living together and when I'd lived in Perth. We were all bound by obligation before I left for Sydney. That didn't mean we didn't love each other, but it didn't mean we shared time together just for the sheer enjoyment of each other's company.

Now things were different. Mum and Laura were changed people. Laura had become her own adult, forging her way in the world after finishing her degree in stage management. Mum was changed also, in a way that would impress me over and over and over again.

Mum was devastated by Dad's departure, but also liberated by it. She didn't see it as an opportunity to be with someone else. Instead she saw it as an opportunity to live her own life, have her own thoughts, engage with any friends she chose, and indulge her passion for history books, black-and-white movies, galleries and theatre.

I was first surprised by her when, after we saw the film *Being John Malkovich* together, I expected the lights to go up and to hear about how much she hated it but instead heard words of admiration and a considered treatise on surrealist art. Mum impressed me then and continues to impress now.

In hospital, Mum and Laura were the cotton wool that wrapped me in my rawest hours, but also a reminder of how much of our relationship was yet to be revealed and how much I'd gained by surviving.

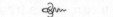

Dad arrived to visit me in hospital some time in my shuffling period. It wasn't the first time I'd seen him since he'd left Mum and our family, but it may have been the first time he'd come to me.

Dad had set up a whole life in Victoria. He and Marlene had bought a restaurant and bar outside of Bendigo called Pratty's Patch.

He just started a new life, with a new partner, new friends and a new industry. He set fire to his old life and to me this had seemed so sudden and harsh.

I had visited them in Victoria a few times but spent every minute itching to leave. I was angry at Dad. Angry at what he'd done, the way he'd done it and the fact he'd never explain to my sister and I why he had cut and run.

I was also angry that I'd never asked him about it either. It just wasn't in me.

I wanted Dad to suffer consequences for what he had

done. But all I could manage was mild detachment and intermittent passive aggression.

I can't imagine he loved my visits too much either. He kept inviting me, though, and I kept going.

So when Dad showed up in the hospital, I appreciated it. I knew he would have been embarrassed, being in such close proximity to Mum and the family. Embarrassment was something Dad avoided the way most people avoid a rabid dog. But he came to see me.

If I knew one Dad in Perth and another in Victoria, then a third arrived to see me in hospital. This Dad seemed older and more vulnerable. Seeing his son so thin and sick would have been a factor, but the arrival of his old friend Steve in hospital was likely another.

I knew Dad and Steve had had a monumental falling out years before. According to Dad, the separation was because Dad had made a joke about one of Steve's children or grandchildren.

Dad and Steve's relationship was defined by a sort of joyful nihilism – one of our family Christmas traditions was listening to Dad on the phone with Steve as they merrily listed the famous people who'd died in the preceding year.

I can imagine this 'nothing matters' attitude was part of a childhood coping mechanism Dad and Steve developed when life wasn't so kind to them. Nothing matters except, of course, each other; a caveat never to be spoken out loud but checked in on every so often by agreeing together that nothing *else* matters.

My dad could be insensitive but not cruel. He never would have genuinely made a disparaging comment about a member of Steve's family, but after the words were said and Steve responded with anger, both prideful men were stuck. I can imagine the disconnection would have hurt both men and made their childhood scars ache, but the disconnection would have been more comfortable than having to pick up the phone and call the other.

Steve may have contacted Dad after hearing about what had happened to me. Then I suspect Dad may have even gone to the extreme measure of apologising to Steve.

Whatever happened, they both turned up at my hospital ward together and the three of us sat on uncomfortable chairs in the recreation nook as ghosts pushing IV drip stands floated past the door. I was very content sitting there as the pair nattered like kids. I was happy for Dad, happy for Steve and, besides, I didn't really have the energy to join in.

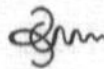

After ten days in hospital, I took my new cardiac scar home under neat and clean bandages, gauze and tape. The scar felt alien and demanding. Sometimes it felt hot, sometimes it wanted to be scratched, sometimes it seemingly wanted to leap off my body. Sometimes I had dreams in which I'd peel the scar off my chest like a long string of red liquorice.

After a week at home, I was allowed to take the dressing off and shower. When I did, I saw in the bathroom mirror an angry red stripe bisecting my breastbone, from abdomen to throat. Initially I hated that scar. I didn't want an inescapable reminder of the heart attack and surgery. I didn't want a constant reminder of my mortality. I also didn't want the constant ticking of the new valve, which even other people could hear when I was in a quiet setting.

I was told that, with a little time and some vitamin E cream, the cardiac scar would settle down to become a thin white line that was barely noticeable. That never became the case. My scar stayed fat, red and angry for years. For months, a hole atop my scar the size of half a marble stayed open, sometimes weeping yellow and red tears.

For years, I had an unconscious reaction to anything touching my scar, especially the top of the scar. When a girlfriend would accidentally touch it, my limbic system would go into overdrive and I'd practically leap off the couch or out of bed.

I couldn't stand the feeling of a seam against the scar, especially the top of my scar, so I wore high necked t-shirts when at home, button-ups open to the sternum when out and I went shirtless at the beach. This meant exposure. This meant a gnarly red line across my chest becoming part of my personal aesthetic. When I was sick and thin and feeling sorry for myself, I hated people looking at the scar, but it was better than feeling uncomfortable.

As my body and soul strengthened, my attitude to the scar changed. I realised that there was no point hating it and, in fact, there was every reason to love it.

A scar is the body sending tissue to where damage has been done to the dermis so the damage can be protected and repaired. It's like friends or family flocking to you with food in a time of need or despair. A scar is your body caring for you. A scar lingers as a memory of that care. A scar is growth. A scar is a permanent story. A scar is also skin. That thing on my chest wasn't just mine, it was me: past, present and future.

After my surgery, I'd been told that I'd improve every day if I kept walking and kept up hope. I kept walking and kept up hope, but I didn't improve.

In the days after getting home, I started to lose the small amount of breath I had when I left St Vincent's Hospital. Having never had open-heart surgery before, I didn't know what to expect from my recovery and didn't call Dr Spratt's rooms until, a couple of weeks after leaving hospital, I attempted to walk the slight hill from my apartment to a coffee shop on Bondi Road and fell exhausted onto a bench about forty metres from my door.

I called Dr Spratt's rooms and was told he'd call back shortly. When he called back, he told me to go to the hospital immediately where he'd meet me.

I was admitted to a ward and, as soon as my vitals were tested, there was an explosion of activity. Dr Spratt appeared and coolly but urgently gave orders to a couple of offsiders. He then told me that something called a pericardial effusion had created an acute cardiac tamponade in my heart and that it needed to be rectified by a procedure. Immediately, on this ward.

He also gave it to me in layman's terms: my heart was bleeding into the sac that surrounds the heart. That blood was choking my heart and with each pump there was an increasing amount of cardiac stress. Untreated, one of these pumps would eventually create a state of cardiac shock. Serious complications.

Screens were erected around my bed, machines were attached to my arms and my chest was painted with a strong-smelling antiseptic solution. Dr Spratt disappeared to prepare for the procedure and I was alone for a quiet moment.

Dr Spratt returned with his sleeves rolled up, two nurses and a tray of implements. The procedure was quick but felt very strange. Dr Spratt made an incision below my sternum then put a long, metal drain into my chest cavity, piercing the pericardium. He then drew out the blood and fluid. A surgeon is truly a mechanic of the body.

The most notable aspect of the procedure was the amount of fluid he drew from my chest. It seemed to be an endless red, viscous river. I was later told it was two and a half litres of fluid.

I felt better immediately after the procedure. It was almost worth having a pericardial effusion just to feel the immense relief of it being resolved. I could breathe. I felt alive.

With that off my chest, my recovery started in earnest. Only a week later, I was on a treadmill, sweating. I'd come back to hospital for a rehabilitation session and, with my heart being monitored constantly, I was pushed into a brisk walk and then a slow run. I hadn't run since I was trying to catch that bus all those months ago, nor had I ever experienced a release of endorphins like the one that flushed my body then.

I allowed myself to drift on a warm wind of joy and hope. Was it possible that everything would actually be okay? I cried with happiness as a circle of sweat grew from the middle of my long, red cardiac scar. Although I was slowly jogging nowhere, it felt like I was sprinting back into life.

I left the hospital feeling hopeful and ready for the rehab that would take me back to health. When I got home, I opened an email from Defence telling me that my request to be embedded with the Australian Defence Force in Iraq had been approved.

I cursed my bad luck. I was too weak, too thin, too sick to go to Iraq. I'd barely been out of the house in months and I had just been administered a life-saving emergency procedure.

I had a scheduled check-up with Dr Spratt a few days later and decided to wait to respond to Defence until after that appointment. Surely Dr Spratt was going to close the door on the possibility of me going to Iraq.

'Will there be much exercise involved in the embed?' Dr Spratt asked.

I told him that was probably wasn't in the ADF plan.

Dr Spratt stared at me for a moment. His mind was working as his face rested. He asked how badly I wanted to go. I told him it would mean a lot. I remember word for word what he said next.

'I think you should go and live your life.'

Chapter 8

the bad war

The first stop of my trip to Iraq was to the Randwick Barracks, a short drive from Bondi. I peeled myself out of bed, double-dressed the cardiac wound that was still bleeding, put on a high-neck thermal I'd bought for the trip and dragged my way to the pre-deployment briefing, meeting journalists from Channel 7, 2GB Radio and *The Australian* newspaper who I'd be travelling with.

The most memorable moment in the briefing was a short session on what to do if we were kidnapped, with the briefer telling us what identifying information we should give so that the SAS would be able to exfiltrate the right person should we be beaten so badly that we couldn't be identified visually.

I left the briefing thinking nothing of the prospect of being kidnapped and beaten, or worse, and everything to do with the prospect of my heart failing while in the field.

We'd been asked to provide medical information and for a moment I considered giving them the information that would undoubtedly disqualify me.

I couldn't be truthful. After meeting with Dr Spratt, the idea of going to Iraq was intertwined with my recovery, physically and emotionally. I saw the trip as a gate, entering it as someone who was sick and broken and exiting as a young man ready to start a new life. It was potentially a career threshold also.

When I creatively filled out the initial application form, however, I didn't have thoughts of recovery or career, but of curiosity. I'd thought so much about that war, read millions of words about it. I had to see what it looked like, or at least what the ADF would reveal to civilians.

Later, when I was working more closely with Australian special forces soldiers, I realised my falsehoods in that medical report were similar to what so many of them did so they could keep deploying to Afghanistan after they had suffered serious mental health breakdowns but were by then addicted to combat.

The Iraqi embed was an incredible experience, but not for the reasons I had imagined it would be.

The trip started dramatically enough: we flew to Diego Garcia, a military airbase dominating a tiny island in the Indian Ocean, then on to a massive American base in Kuwait.

There, we were issued helmets, ballistic vests and battlefield medical kits, before loading up on a C-17 Hercules for what was then called the 'Brown Route' into Iraq. After a corkscrew touch-and-go landing in Baghdad, we flew on to Talil airbase in Dhi Qar Governorate, where an Australian Battle Group was stationed.

The area was almost exclusively populated by Shi'ites and in Iraq this group, the majority sect, had been marginalised and persecuted by Saddam Hussein and the minority Sunnis.

In the wake of the American invasion, Sunni radicals and former Ba'athists, the group who had controlled the country for and with Saddam Hussein, were wreaking havoc to the north and north-west, attacking coalition forces and the new Shi'ite government, but in Dhi Qar they had little or no presence. The primary threat in this area were Shi'ite militias, including the Badr Brigade, who fought alongside Iran in the Iran–Iraq war in the 1980s. These groups sometimes attacked Western forces under orders from tribal heads, but not as a matter of routine.

The area was actually far safer than most parts of Iraq and Afghanistan, and even then the embed was something of a walled garden experience.

After settling into our quarters in a tent in the Australian section of the giant American base, we were given a tour of the facilities. The base had more comforts and facilities than most small towns enjoy, with a Burger King, McDonald's and Baskin-Robbins (I was told the Baskin-Robbins in Basra had opened before the US forces had even reached Baghdad). There was also a cinema and Harley Davidson and Ford showrooms.

There were a lot of US soldiers on the base, but their number was dwarfed by the number of contractors. These were mostly Nepalese, Bangladeshi and Indian, doing menial tasks, but there were also hundreds of Halliburton and Kellogg Brown & Root private military contractors: modern-day Wyatt Earps wearing brown pants or jeans, t-shirts covering gym muscles, boots, wrap-around sunglasses, ballistic vests and carrying a rifle and sidearm.

Fighter jets, transporters and helicopters flew in and out of the base all day. Delivery men on pushbikes ferried fast food around a tent city the size of Newcastle. Contractors and soldiers milled waiting for orders. The scope and commercialisation of the war was stunning.

I had a thought that started in Iraq and strengthened as I learned more – there is no better way to transfer billions of dollars from public coffers to private pockets than via a war.

The Australian base was a tiny part of the American network; a modular part of a massive American whole.

Ostensibly, the Australian role in Iraq was to support federal Iraqi forces, should they need support, particularly vehicle support. But the Australian force of primarily conventional forces and cavalry were never used in that capacity. We were told the Australians were also engaging with local tribal elders, and undertaking reconstruction projects within the province but, for the first part of the embed, we didn't see it.

The other journalists and I mostly spent our days inside the wire doing interviews, getting briefings and shooting different type of weapons on the range. We also went out on a vehicle range with a detachment of Australian Light Armoured Vehicles, or ASLAV, and Bushmaster fighting vehicles, watching the vehicles manoeuvre and fire at static targets. We visited the nearby Ziggurat of Ur, an incredible neo-Sumerian structure of great cultural importance, first built in the twenty-first century BCE, which was some kilometres from the base but had been claimed by the

Americans because, from it, the centre of the base could be seen. Some of us were flown in a Blackhawk to visit one of the Australian ships protecting Iraq's on-water oil export facilities.

These were all fascinating experiences, and ideal stops on a risk-averse trip of war-tourism, but we'd had very few interactions with Iraqis and my curiosity wouldn't be sated without those.

The other journalists I was touring with seemed fine with this, as they had captured plenty of dramatic footage, but I was hoping we'd be there for the engagements with local tribal heads, go into the nearby city of Nasiriyah and do a little barbershop reporting. I wanted to understand how the locals were feeling about the Americans and their little friends, the Australians. I wanted to understand better the Sadrists, the Badr brigade and the other Iranian-backed militias. I wanted to understand what the military call the human terrain.

When we arrived in Iraq we had been welcomed by an Australian lieutenant colonel who was in charge of Australian forces in Dhi Qar. He'd told us to let him know personally if there was anything we needed during our trip so one night I asked the other journalists if they wanted to join me in asking the colonel whether we may get out of the base a little more and meet some Iraqis where they lived and find out if they were benefiting from Australia's reconstruction efforts.

The reporter from Channel 7 came with me to visit the colonel with our request. The colonel told me it would require some work, but he'd see what he could do.

He was good to his word. The next morning, we left in a large convoy of ASLAVs, Bushmasters and Iraqi Hilux utes with heavy machine guns bolted into the tray after condemning some Australian soldiers to a long night of planning, preparing and signal jamming.

We visited a number of sites, which included a village of mudhifs, the traditional dwelling of the Madan or the Marsh Arabs on the Euphrates River. This was a cultural and ethnic group who had resisted Saddam, especially in 1991 after the First Gulf War. While the group we visited wasn't part of the uprising, they were subject to the retributions that followed, with Saddam's forces attacking their villages and others nearby. Through an interpreter, one of the elders and I spoke for a while about their experiences in the 1990s, and about the changes they'd seen since 2003 which, he said, were minimal. They hated Saddam and were glad he was gone, but they were largely disconnected from government. This was seemingly true of all the places we visited, except at the large villa of a local sheik, who hosted us and a US senior officer for dinner.

We were placed near the foot of the long dinner mat, with some of the sheik's young cousins. These men were Sadrists, showing me pictures on their phones of them, guns in hand, at a rally with Muqtada al-Sadr, Iraq's most prominent and volatile Shi'ite cleric.

I asked how they felt about the Americans and they said they didn't care about them. They were happy the Americans had removed Saddam and they'd take anything the Americans would give them. They'd take anything the Australians had to give also, but the Americans and the Australians and the British, and whomever else, were just here today and gone tomorrow. The Americans were no longer a factor. They didn't matter. Sects, tribes and family were what mattered.

After a meal of whole spiced sheep baked in fruit and spices and then splayed out on rice, one of the cousins took me by the hand so we could wash our hands at a fountain nearby. We had been sitting on the floor of a gazebo under overhead fluorescent lights and when we moved a few metres from the table toward a marble sink, we were in nearly pitch darkness.

As my eyes adjusted to the dark, I could see some shadows moving around us. I could just make out a person, wearing night-vision equipment, scanning the night with his suppressed M4 pulled to his shoulder. This was one of a group of Australian special forces operators – men literally in the shadows – pulling personal security detail. It was thrilling, seeing these famed figures at work. I knew little about Australia's special forces then but I'd been reading about the British, American and Israeli special forces pretty much since I finished my last Tom Clancy book.

I left Iraq shortly afterwards, thinking that Australia had roughly got it right. The Iraq War had been a mistake and the Americans had neither the will nor patience to create a civil society here. They were loved by no one nor did they have any moral mandate as the war was run by the military and agencies like the CIA. Iraq needed to heal, but most of the American tools available in that effort were lethal.

There was danger in these aimless post-9/11 wars, not only bodily but moral. I'd seen that moral danger in Iraq, when travelling in a Bushmaster and seeing a dented and heavy axe handle with 'BAD SMOOFTY' written on it. And while having coffee with two New Zealand contractors who had just come back from Route Tampa, the main north–south supply route in Iraq, and casually mentioned they'd executed two young boys they found trying to lay an IED.

Australia had supported the Americans in the wake of 9/11 but had managed to largely stay out of the bodies and hatred game. I believed we were a lucky nation because of it.

Australian forces in Iraq were tucked away in the Shi'ite-dominated south of Iraq, and in Afghanistan the Australian military, we were told, were in a relatively permissive environment having replaced the shooters of Australia's Special Forces Task Group with a Reconstruction Task Force of engineers, nurses and builders.

My opinion, that Australia was mostly away from the physical and moral danger of this war, was reflected in the pieces I wrote about my embed, for *The Bulletin* magazine, the *West Australian* newspaper and *Ralph*.

As I wrote my first, serious and potentially even newsworthy piece for *The Bulletin*, I did so with caution and even sometimes a sense of fear. I had some drafts including copy reflecting interactions with the Marsh Arabs and the Sadrists which spoke about the sideshow-of-a-sideshow and there-to-win-a-participation-trophy nature of Australia's role in America's war, but those paragraphs were never sent.

I didn't feel confident writing about how Australia's commitment in Iraq related to the larger geopolitical picture. I never would have considered writing in that context, except that the journalists I travelled with had such a poor understanding of the country and the conflict.

One didn't even understand there was a difference between the Sunni and Shi'ite faiths and none knew any of the historical context of the war.

After talking to the Marsh Arabs about their failed uprising, a well-known defence correspondent from a Murdoch paper asked me why I knew so much about Iraq. I wanted to ask why he knew so little, central as the conflict seemed to be to the current Australian military experience.

I didn't ask him that, though, and ended up writing a piece that was primarily about the Australian soldiers I met, all of whom were happy to be deployed and all of whom were comfortable or agnostic about Australia's involvement with the invasion and the war.

I was surprised when Prime Minister John Howard quoted my story in parliament. I couldn't help but be a little proud. After all, to the best of my knowledge, none of my *Ralph* articles had ever been mentioned in parliament, federal or state, or even in local councils. I suspected that this was the closest I'd get to 'proper' journalism, so it was gratifying to get some kind of 'proper' response.

Seeing John Howard quote selectively as he did was also frustrating. He was using my work in support of an egregious argument that persists to this day – that the invasion was a good idea and that the decision to commit Australia to the invasion and the war was a good one.

I had strong feelings about the Iraq War, and all the death and social, political and legal changes that were happening in the wake of 9/11. I had strong feelings about Australians being involved in wars that we had no business being involved in.

I hoped that one day those feelings might be fully represented in work that I did, even though I had little belief attached to that hope.

After the Iraq trip, I kept up a freelance career for a few hectic years. I spent between a half and third of the year travelling; a four-month stint in Beijing working on the Olympics there, five wonderful weeks in Iran working on a piece for *Rolling Stone*, a few weeks in Lebanon, Hong Kong, London, Oslo, Tokyo, Mexico City, Vancouver, and countless trips to Los Angeles and New York, often courtesy of work I was doing covering video games for Telstra's content team.

I also spent a couple of dusty weeks in Kabul at a time when the Iraq conflict was considered the 'Bad War' in comparison to Afghanistan's 'Good War'. The city was relatively safe and, travelling just with a driver/interpreter and no bodyguard, I fell into the trap of believing the calm of the capital represented the mood of the country.

Even when speaking to Afghans who told me that they had no doubt the Taliban would rule the country again, I considered them strangely pessimistic. So too when they laughed at the prospect of Australian troops working in Uruzgan province in a permissive situation, which is how Defence was describing the situation to the Australian public.

I was in Afghanistan to write about a skate park and school built in Kabul by a Melbourne skater. I never presumed it would be worthwhile for me to investigate what was really happening in Uruzgan.

At the time, my work was good enough to get more work but rarely better than that. I wasn't in it for the work then, though – I was in it for the experiences. As a writer, I was uncertain of my ability before my stroke and heart attack, and afterwards, I refused to believe that the experience had improved my capabilities on the page.

There were lingering effects of the brain damage that expressed themselves in my speech and writing. I mixed tenses, became lost in clauses, misplaced words and I was a grammatical liability; I still feel these effects today, especially when I'm tired or overwhelmed.

I believed there were hard limits on my career and that I'd essentially reached them. That was okay, though. I was alive and I had carved out a post-*Ralph* career. I liked my life and I liked my work. As my new heart valve ticked away and counted down the seconds of my life, I was okay with a career in which I only really enriched myself matching the life that only enriched myself.

I would have liked to have been able to write something that had true value for the reader. I would have liked to transpose the strong emotions and feelings I felt onto the page and then into the reader's psyche. I just didn't think I was capable of doing it. Until it happened.

Part II

Chapter 9

born to fight

In 2010, I had a job and a girlfriend, two pinch grips from which I could have scrambled my way towards being a normal property-owning, newish-car-driving and potentially even child-rearing mature adult.

I considered myself lucky to have both. Although they were both somewhat ill-fitting. By 2015, I had neither.

The job was with Fairfax Media, then the most respected media organisation in the country, primarily because they published the *Sydney Morning Herald* and *The Age* newspapers.

After a series of interviews, including with the company's CEO who, I was impressed to find, approved all senior editorial positions, I was hired as the editor of *Sport&Style*, the glossy magazine inserted monthly into the *Sydney Morning Herald* and *The Age*.

It was a great job. I had an exceptionally talented little team, an insightful publisher and a job asking me to pull together a magazine that was relatively slight in heft, but well considered in every word and image.

At the centre of each issue were two or three long reads, usually athlete profiles accompanied by lavish fashion shoots. From local heroes like Mark Webber, Liesel Jones, Sam Stosur, Anthony Mundine and Tim Cahill, to international blue-chippers like Serena Williams, Shaun White and LeBron James, it was the highest quality magazine I had worked on, and I loved that the role allowed me to conceive and produce each issue, but also write at least one of the profiles.

This was my favourite part of the job. So often when working as a journalist, you're looking for information when interviewing, or even searching for quotes or comments that fit into a story that you've already written in your head.

When writing profiles, I was looking for an honest connection, from which an emotional truth could be exposed. I wanted the subject to tell me something about themselves that was unique and deeply felt, hopefully something that spoke to the reason they had been chosen to be profiled in the first place.

Sometimes it starts with a personal connection, like the fact that Mark Webber was born in the same hospital that I was, or that Shaun White was born with a congenital heart defect that required open-heart surgery, or that Anthony Mundine and I had shared the same boxing trainer. Sometimes it's simply proving that you can listen and empathise, and you're not just rushing to get the subject to tell you what you want to hear.

If you're lucky, you will get to a point where you're no longer interviewing, you're connecting, not hearing rote answers already awash on the internet, but connecting and considering the subject's life and life itself.

These profiles were also important for my career. They were some of the first articles I wasn't fearful of people reading because I knew they represented something significant, which was that myself and Tim Cahill or Shaun White had spoken honestly and truly, even if only for a short while. Without those profiles, I would have found the first books I wrote even more challenging than they were. Perhaps too challenging.

In 2012, the plug was pulled on the company's entire magazine division, with only the *Good Weekend* supplement staying in the editorial sink. That was the harsh world of magazine work in Australia (so harsh now, it barely exists).

Afterwards, Peter Fray, the editor of the *Sydney Morning Herald*, took me into his office and asked me whether I would like to take a redundancy or move to the staff of the paper as the senior features writer.

I took the job and found it inspiring but also difficult. I'd been catapulted onto the senior desk of a paper that was downsizing every day. The people who worked around me were smart and hardworking but also undeniably protective of their patches. After a year at the paper, I was taken into a different editor's office during one of many rounds of redundancies and was asked whether I'd like to take a pay cut or a voluntary redundancy.

Throughout all of this and through the freelance years, I'd been in a relationship with a talented and ambitious media executive who worked in television. It was a full-time relationship fulfilled on a part-time schedule, which had mostly suited both of us. I had been away a lot working but she also worked very long hours.

When I was at Fairfax, I was in Sydney more often than I had been when I'd been chasing freelance stories, but our hours hadn't changed much. Often she said that she wanted, at some point, for both of our lives to settle. She had envisioned a future that looked like her past – children in private school uniforms, a husband pulling an expensive car into a big suburban house. I was paid pretty well at Fairfax and would still be paid decently if I took the pay cut. I'd go to work in the morning, come home in the afternoon and be at home on weekends, and every two weeks money would arrive in our account. It was reasonable for her to want that of me and for us.

I suppose that relationship was doomed when I took the redundancy.

About a dozen journalists at Fairfax were doing important and ground-breaking work, and the rest were filling the paper up. I had started my newspaper career in my thirties and would always be in the latter category. I wasn't a newspaper journalist and if my newspaper career wasn't caught in this redundancy net, it would be in the next, or the next.

Every few weeks, people were packing their desks up. Every few weeks, a cheap cadet replaced a senior journalist. Every few months, Sydney's Google offices took another floor of the building, the company literally eating the print media piece by piece.

I was still looking for something that wouldn't be found at Fairfax's increasingly depressing offices. I wanted more excitement, more adventure, more of the one thing I'd identified that I was good at – creating a place where a subject who'd had extreme experiences could talk to me about things that were significant to them.

That wasn't the job at the *Sydney Morning Herald*. I got a sense that that had been the job, perhaps some time ago, when Fairfax's foreign bureaus still existed, but that wasn't the job now.

I just wasn't a newsman.

I met with a book publisher, someone who I'd come to know after sending a very early idea for this book to her a couple of years before. We talked about a few potential projects and then the possibility of me co-authoring books – writing someone else's biography in their voice, with my name in small font sitting below their larger font name.

I wasn't against the idea. I generally didn't read many biographies, but I thought it was something that I could maybe do.

The publisher suggested a book about an Ultimate Fighting Championship (UFC) fighter. She wasn't a fan of the sport but knew I was and that it was becoming increasingly popular in Australia. I mentioned the only appropriate candidate for a biography would be Mark Hunt.

A giant, tattooed Sāmoan fighter who'd been born in New Zealand, Mark Hunt was then in the middle of an incredible UFC *Cinderella Man* run. After having success in the K-1 Kickboxing Championships and Pride Fighting Championships, two hugely popular, Yakuza-run Japanese martial arts organisations, Hunt had moved to the UFC and then promptly went on a losing streak. The organisation had famously tried hard to sack him, but he took them to court so he could keep fighting. And then he started to win. That was his sporting story. I didn't know his life story. No one did, really. Mark had never talked about his personal life.

My first interview session with Mark was at a coffee shop in the food court at the Macarthur Square shopping centre in Western Sydney. Mark's manager and the publisher had spent a long time getting Mark to agree to the book, so when Mark and I finally sat down we had only three months to deliver the manuscript. I wanted to start at the beginning, so I asked him to tell me about his parents.

Mark had nothing to say about them, and after I had posed that question he had nothing to say at all. He locked up. I sat there asking questions and he sat there, mostly silent and obviously frustrated. I wondered what would happen if this 140-kilogram ball of muscle snapped and launched over the Formica table at me, scattering cookies, cappuccinos and me this way and that.

Mark quickly left but agreed to a second session at the same café. This time, Mark brought a friend: a very large, very chatty Tongan man named Tunga.

Mark and Tunga played speed chess, a game Mark had learned while in prison, and as they did, Tunga spoke incessantly. I tried to put questions to Mark, this time asking about school and his siblings, but it was hard to penetrate Tunga's wall of chat. Eventually I asked if Mark and I could just talk alone.

'Okay, yeah. Just one sec,' Mark said, walking off.

I assumed he was going to the bathroom.

About ten minutes later, I interjected into one of Tunga's stories to ask him whether Mark was coming back.

'Mark?' Tunga said in his soft lilt, looking in the direction his friend had gone and then pausing for an uncharacteristic period of time.

'No, I wouldn't think so.' He then continued chatting apace.

I enticed Mark for a third session, telling him I was only going to ask him questions about his fighting career. He was still guarded and short in the interview, because I think he knew the question of his childhood was going to arise somehow, some time.

When I was about to leave, I brought it up. 'We have to say something about your childhood, even if it's an explanation that you don't want to say anything about your childhood,' I said.

Mark was prepared. He told me again that he didn't remember anything, but he also gave me a scrap of paper with a name and number.

The name was Victoria. She was the eldest of four Hunt children, followed by John, Steve and finally Mark, the baby.

'My sister remembers better,' Hunt said.

I called Victoria but the number was disconnected. I found her on Facebook, where I introduced myself and told her I was hoping to visit her while in Auckland, a city Mark and I were about to go to so he could train at City Kickboxing gym.

Victoria was largely estranged from Mark and wary, but she said I could visit her.

When I arrived in Auckland, I rented a car and drove to Victoria's South Auckland home, purchased outright from one of Mark's first large purses in the early 2000s. Victoria, then in her fifties, lived in the house with their brother Steve, who was much larger than his heavyweight brother, schizophrenic and largely non-verbal. John, the eldest of the Hunt boys, had also lived in the house, but had taken his own life a year prior.

Over two hours, Victoria proceeded to tell me the horrific story of her childhood and her tormentor and father, Charles.

Charles had been a 'freshie', a fresh-off-the-boat Sāmoan, and he'd stayed a freshie his whole life, even decades after he'd moved to New Zealand. He made few connections outside of his extended family and the Mormon church he worshipped at. He also made little effort to learn English. He was a prideful and rageful man who was sometimes out of work and often in debt. And he abused his children.

Charles beat the boys very badly and raped his daughter, a sin that started when she was about nine and later became a daily after-school ritual. Mark's mother offered no protection to her children, laughing about the abuse and telling the boys not to go into the bedroom when Dad was 'having his fun'. After the rapes, Charles washed himself in Dettol and demanded his dinner.

Victoria told me about a time when Charles was out of work and the children were starving. She and the other Hunt kids were sent to Sāmoa. She thought she'd find relief there but instead she was habitually raped by her uncle in what, it seems, was a generational practice.

In her early teens, Victoria briefly fell pregnant to her father. Charles did a short stint in gaol after Victoria started to show, but after she had an abortion and he fulfilled his sentence, the abuse continued.

Victoria told me her story in a very matter-of-fact way, except in a few instances when tears escaped her granite face. When that happened, I asked if she wanted to stop. In each instance, she said she wanted to keep going.

At the end of it all, I thanked her and she told me it had felt good to talk. I got into my hire car and looked at the dry grey sky. My stomach turned and I cried and cried and cried.

I went back to my hotel and started writing. Afterwards, when I wasn't writing, I was following Mark around as best I could, sitting in as he trained or when he ate, trying to pick up his way of speaking and the nuances in his vocabulary.

I rushed out a first draft of a first chapter in a little more than a week, messaging Victoria and asking her if she'd like to read what I'd written before it went to Mark. She asked if I'd written what she said and I said I had. She said she didn't need to read it.

I met Mark at the studio apartment he'd rented in central Auckland and there I read out to him what I had written. A quote from my interview with Victoria starts the book:

> Mark was still a baby when all hell broke loose. He'd be black and blue head to toe regularly. I'd have to wash away the blood, massage the bruises and put salt on his wounds, so his dad can give him another beating. At about five Mark started to become a thief and a violent maniac, but how would he know any better? He didn't even understand what love was until he met Julie (Mark's wife). There were good parts of him but, that survived the abuse. Those parts became the soul of my brother.

Afterwards, I'd written a short history of Mark's parents before, with the scene set, we moved behind young Mark's eyes.

I can still see the dark Auckland room, strewn with boxing equipment and Jean-Claude Van Damme DVDs, in which I read that chapter to Mark. I darted a look over to him from time to time as I read. Each time, he was staring at the roof. Sometimes I stopped reading, often after a description of abuse, to see if he wanted to continue.

'Yeah, go on,' he said each time.

That first chapter ends with a moment of confrontational kindness. When she was a teen, Victoria took an after-school job, primarily to get away from what was happening after the school bell. Her pay went to her father, but she managed to siphon away a small amount of money every week for an escape fund. One day, she'd earned enough to rent a room on the other side of Auckland. She tried to leave the house with her belongings, but Charles was home when she hadn't expected him to be. He was furious and wasn't going to allow her to leave.

Her brothers intervened. John, Steve and even ten-year-old Mark. Normally the brothers just took their beatings when they came, as teaming up or fighting back would only create more pain. Not today. Charles laughed at these boys, perhaps nervously as two were going through puberty and had become dangerously large. There was no brawl and Victoria left. The end of the chapter explains that Victoria's life wasn't easy after that but that she survives to this day. Given the circumstances she grew up in, that's something.

When I finished the chapter, Mark seemed energised, even happy. I still remember exactly what he said to me.

'That's what happened. It's good the way you've done it. You say the words and you're in that place and you can see the things happening. It's like being there.'

I wondered if anyone had ever read any of the Hunt kids a story before.

After that, Mark opened up to me. He'd only ever spoken to his wife about his childhood, but he was ready to have all the pus and infection drawn away from his mind and onto the page.

We spent all of Mark's spare time in Auckland together, talking about his darkest secrets.

Mark and I went back to his childhood house in South Auckland and, there, memories poured from him: feelings and smells that prompted stories. We drove around the streets where Mark fought, where he robbed people and where he stole cars. We went to the place where he first suffered psychosis, seeing the devil appear. In the book, those moments were presented not as a man looking back at the deliria of his past, but as his reality. The finished book starts with Charles Hunt's death. Mark was there, at the hospital. According to Mark, the devil was there too, to take his father's soul away. Mark bowed his head to the devil as his father passed. So be it.

When working with Mark, I thought a lot about the power of story and the misleading nature of perception.

Mark is not someone who is seen as an intellectual. At the time, his refusal to give much more than one-word answers in post-fight interviews had become a meme in MMA fandom, and not one that was very kind.

Mark is a smart and considered man, in particular contexts, and always thinking. There were two elements that had limited people's ability to see Mark for who he was. One was his limited ability for articulation, a skill that was not honed in his school years, and the other was his inability to have his emotional ducks fully lined up at times as they should have been, which is a very benign way to describe the nature of trauma.

American writer Joan Didion wrote once that we tell ourselves stories in order to survive and that 'especially if we are writers, by the imposition of a narrative line upon disparate images, by the ideas with which we have learned to freeze the shifting phantasmagoria which is our actual experience'.

Trauma is when we can't find the sermon or the social and moral lesson. Trauma is what happens when we can't tell ourselves a story, and yet our lives continue regardless.

Trauma is, by its definition, something our psyche is not equipped to cope with and so it cannot be incorporated into the story we tell ourselves about ourselves. It's not something we can recognise the shape of, nor are we able to predict its effects, yet it's a piercing scream in a symphony; a blast of light on developing film.

Intrusive memories and unprocessed thoughts about Mark's childhood infected so many interactions in his life, and informed so many of his outcomes. Mark didn't recognise his trauma, he felt it only as shame.

Trauma changes us. Often, after a traumatic event, our previously held beliefs and assumptions are tested. What was believed to have been the bedrock of our life may have been proven to be soft fudge. The immovable foundations of life – religion, philosophy, morality, cultural norms – may start to shake. Once those foundations are rocked, life can change. Often for the worse, but not always. Trauma can be a superpower, by exploding expectations and limitations.

Trauma, especially childhood trauma, can create a preternatural, perhaps even antisocial, focus.

Mark Hunt's childhood trauma almost certainly contributed to him developing coping mechanisms that would help him become the fighter that he is. They also may have contributed to 'stunting personality growth and producing the concomitant antisocial acts, destruction of social relationships, and even the [thoughts of] taking one's own life', as researcher Dr J Marvin Eisenstadt wrote in a paper about childhood trauma and adult exceptionality.

While working with Mark, I learned a lot about the links between trauma, the story we tell about ourselves and our actions.

I mostly thought about Mark's story and his trauma while working on his book, but I sometimes thought about mine too.

I'd never considered myself as experiencing trauma before, and yet my depressive events, stroke and heart attack were all examples of trauma. Each had affected me and changed me. They'd put fear and doubt into me, but also a drive and curiosity.

It occurred to me I was identifying the snakes and ladders of Mark's life, which I believed were borne of trauma, and yet I'd never even tried to do the same for myself.

Both Mark and I took a lot away from the connection that we'd made while working together.

I think he discovered the power of putting borders around a trauma and how storytelling can contain, define and defuse a difficult history. I realised I was never going to be the writer nor person that I had been before I started his book.

Writing a book in someone else's voice wasn't glamourous work, nor did it pay very well, but I found it very gratifying.

I understood Mark in a way I'd never understood anyone I'd written about before. I understood the rage and paranoia of Mark's young adulthood and his unconscious desire to set on fire the good things that had come into his life.

I understood why he fought in a ring and then a cage, where there were only two fists in front of him, two feet, two knees, two elbows. I understood why being locked in a cage with another fighter was a relief for Mark. I understood why Mark didn't feel pain and I understood why he always felt there would be greatness in his life: something that seemed to others like a delusion until it happened.

I understood Mark's incredible three-steps-forward-and-two-back life as a fighter and as a man because Mark had already done so much of the work. Mark had already questioned his motivations and investigated his life. I think he understood when he was hurting people, something he had done in his life to the people he loved. I think he wanted to know why he was doing that, and how to stop doing it. He'd refused to reason his actions away, ignore them or to identify simply as a bad person who did bad things.

Before we even sat down for that first meeting, Mark had stopped hurting people, except those who were paid for the privilege. He was hurting still, but not the people around him.

Through the maddest circumstances, Mark had fostered and fed a flickering moral flame, one that illuminated our interviews. This flame was the difference between Charles Hunt and his son, and the reason *Born to Fight* became such a good book.

I enjoyed every aspect of writing *Born to Fight* – both the interviews and putting the story on the page. I just wrote down what happened, sparsely and with little embellishment. The story often soared in a way nothing I'd written before had.

When it was finished, I took the manuscript to Mark with some trepidation. Mark's wife read the book to Mark, as he lay on the bed and looked at the ceiling, and then she read it to him again. He then texted me: 'Algud. That's wat happened.'

Later, he told me just how proud he was of the book. It's something I'm very proud of also, as a text but also as a record of an incredible few months in Auckland, Sydney, Melbourne and Las Vegas, with someone who's now a good friend.

After the publication of *Born to Fight*, Mark started the first therapy session of his life – something that continues to this day. Mark's been a different man every day, mending his relationships one by one. The first one he tackled was his adult son Caleb, who Mark apologised to on stage. That shocked everyone who knew Mark, especially Caleb. Then it was Mark's wife, Julie, who is the hero of *Born to Fight*, perhaps more than the protagonist himself. Mark and Julie went through a process of radical recognition, acknowledging that Mark had been using and often abusing Julie's kindness to stay sane and stay alive. It had taken its toll on Julie and they agreed to split, in the most loving and mature way.

They still live together now, with their kids and as best friends, even though they see other people. Mark's therapist told him he had to forgive his mum if he wanted to be able to move on completely. It took years, but he's done that. Mark's now in the process of forgiving his dad, which is something he reckons he'll be doing for some time.

I made a change in my own life after the publication of *Born to Fight*.

My girlfriend didn't particularly like the book or its milieu, nor did she understand why I had to spend all my time with Mark, chasing him around Sydney and the world, when my contract could have been fulfilled with a series of long phone interviews. Her concern was fair, but I had to be with Mark, see his expressions, training sessions and environments. I became intensely and obsessively interested in Mark's life. In the way that I couldn't bear missing out on what Iraq looked like, I had to follow Mark around as we worked.

My girlfriend should have been prioritised over Mark, but she wasn't. As I write this down, it occurs to me that was probably the reason why she didn't like the book nor the milieu.

One night, just after I'd finished *Born to Fight*, she and I were discussing this at a film premiere, waiting for the lights to go down. She asked me if she thought we should break up then. I thought we should. As the lights dimmed, she asked, 'Are you breaking up with me?'

I didn't say anything.

'What am I supposed to do now?' she said. 'Watch the film?'

'We can talk more when it's over,' I said.

'What the fuck is wrong with you?' she asked, then walked out of the movie and out of my life.

I did wonder what the fuck was wrong with me as she walked away. Both as I watched the film and in the days and weeks that followed. This was no way to end a relationship nor treat someone I loved, and yet I couldn't quite envision how things could have gone better.

I've told myself since that the manner of our break-up was largely immaterial. It ended and she was able to quickly find the man and familial circumstance she wanted, while I could move on to an African adventure and a very popular book about a complex man with complex trauma.

Chapter 10

songs of a war boy

In the wake of the release of *Born to Fight*, the publisher of that book arranged for me to have lunch with South Sudanese Australian lawyer Deng Adut, after she'd seen a Western Sydney University advertisement about Deng that she thought could be teased out into a book.

The ad starts with a child in an African village, who is then taken from his mother by guerrillas. It shows his conscription as a child soldier, battle, injury, escape and resettlement in Australia. He is shown as a homeless teen then as an undergraduate studying for a law degree at

Western Sydney University. The advertisement ends with the real Deng Adut winning a case in court. As soon as the judge's gavel falls, an actor playing Deng's mother appears in court. Their eyes connect in a knowing and resolving moment.

Deng arrived to our lunch late but incredibly attired. I would soon learn both things were typical of him. He'd matched his tailored pinstripe suit with a black shirt, colourful silk scarf, trilby hat and Italian leather loafers. Inside the clothes was a thin but muscular man, of above average height here in Australia but short in his native South Sudan.

When he removed his hat, I noticed Deng's forehead was marked with a fountain of scars, from between his eyes towards his hairline. His mother gave him these scars as a baby; a traditional preventative treatment for river blindness. I also saw scars on the back of his head, from shrapnel that seared through him during a battle he participated in when he was perhaps eleven or twelve years of age.

We met roughly two decades after that battle.

At lunch, Deng did most of the talking and was quite forceful, sometimes to the point of being confrontational. He spoke quickly and his accent was thick. I was often trying to catch up. Deng had many demands to do with the sale and rights of the book, and he wanted me to go back to South Sudan with him to retrace his steps through the war.

None of that seemed feasible and I walked away fairly confident the book wasn't happening.

But each day, the publisher called me telling me that they were inching closer to signing a contract with Deng. Deng's unreasonable demands fell away each day with only one remaining: he wanted us to go back to Africa.

I agreed to meet with Deng again, this time in Blacktown, where he was to give a speech at a Rotary Club.

After shaking Deng's hand in the dimly lit hall, I sat down in the mostly older, mostly male Anglo and Asian audience and watched Deng take the microphone and bounce around time and place. One moment we were on the battlefield, next we were in his mother's arms. We were in an Australian courtroom then at a refugee camp. His brother John arrived in the story, then he's mourning his loss and then his brother is with him again. It was breakneck and confusing, but also totally compelling.

These moments were all fresh and affecting and significant to Deng. They were also clearly unresolved and often it seemed to me that Deng was trying to make sense of a moment by talking his way through it. It was as though he hoped an answer to the question in his mind may suddenly come out of his mouth. They never did, though. These were vignettes of an incredibly vibrant but unsettled life, and one that Deng seemed to desperately be trying to make sense of.

My imagination was brimming when I left the Rotary Club. The difficulties and dangers of working on a book with Deng receded in my mind, as the immense possibilities came to the fore.

In George Saunders' book *A Swim in a Pond in the Rain*, he describes a story as 'a system for the transfer of energy. Energy, hopefully, gets made in the early pages and the trick, in the later pages, is to use that energy.'

In a story, that energy is often hope, potential and mystery and it's often then transferred into resolution and meaning. I think similar energy exists in us too, as drive and will but also disquiet or anger. It's anything in us that strives to be released.

There was undoubtedly story energy in Deng Adut. It seemed to vibrate from his skin and I think it was a surplus of story energy that eventually had him sign up to do the book.

There was story energy driving me, also.

In the weeks after signing contracts, Deng and I spent most afternoons together either in Blacktown, where he had a law office, or in Redfern, where he lived. There, we sketched out the story of Deng's many lives.

Born in the 1980s in a tiny, rural village in a unified Sudan, next to the White Nile River, Deng lived a very traditional lifestyle as part of the Dinka people.

At age seven, Deng was taken from his village and family by the Sudanese People's Liberation Army (SPLA), a rebel army of people indigenous to southern Sudan, who were resisting Islam and northern influence. He was one of the Lost Boys of Sudan.

The SPLA taught Deng that his AK-47 rifle and the word of independence leader John Garang were now his mother and father. He was a soldier fighting for the SPLA.

During this time, he saw many of his little friends die, in combat and of disease. He was part of the infamous chase to the Gilo River where hundreds of boys were killed: shot, drowned or eaten by crocodiles. He was blown up and shot at multiple times. Deng was traumatised.

He managed to escape to Kenya as a refugee. From there, he made it to a third country, Australia, where he learned English, completed a high school equivalency, finished a law degree and started working at a law firm. Deng became an Australian and a lawyer.

He reminded me sometimes of Norman Mailer's description of Hunter S. Thompson, so tightly wound that he 'squeaked if you poked a finger near his belly. He was a set of nerves balanced on another set of nerves travelling on squeaky roller skates.' Yet Deng also managed to perpetually maintain a cool, fiery intelligence and a sense of humour that appreciated life's absurdity.

In the gap between writing *Born to Fight* and its publication, I'd accepted a year-long contract to assemble and run a content team for a Sydney university and I was in a pretty comfortable place. I had money coming in, I had a strong foundation of friends and, single for the first time in many years, I was enjoying the liberties and pleasures of single life.

There was a lot to like about the idea of staying in Sydney and working exactly as much as I had to. There were also a lot of reasons not to go with Deng to South Sudan, even though he insisted.

I thought of Canadian Amanda Lindhout, a friend I made in Istanbul as I was waiting for my Syrian visa a few years earlier, and someone I met again later in Sydney and Bali. When I first met Amanda, she was a bartender who dreamed of adventure and being a journalist, a dream she achieved but in a compromised way.

Amanda took work in Baghdad with Press Television, an English-language station wholly funded and controlled by the Iranian Government and whose propaganda I often laughed at while in Iran.

She also went without an assignment and without proper precautions to Somalia, where she was kidnapped, held for more than a year, tortured and raped and, eventually, after a ransom was paid, freed. It was a terrible ordeal for her and her family.

After being released, Sara Corbett, a writer from *The New York Times*, collaborated with Amanda on a million-copy-selling memoir, *A House in the Sky*, whose movie rights were bought by Megan Ellison, but I considered Amanda's story a cautionary tale.

Yet I developed a strong desire to go to South Sudan with Deng. My own story energy was manifesting again as extreme curiosity. I'd never been to Africa and could barely conceive what South Sudan might be like.

I'd seen images of Sudan's old war. The one that Deng had fought in, brutal even by African standards and killing millions. I'd seen images of South Sudan's new war, which was ongoing and made the country one of the most dangerous places on earth. I'd seen pictures of Sudanese

Dinka villages, villagers and their incredible long-horned cattle.

I wanted to see how it all fitted together. I had to see. My decision to accept the risk of the trip – not to mention the cost of flights, secure accommodation, rental satellite phone, insurance and everything else – was because of the story energy that had been collecting ever since that professor of psychology had asked me in the Perth hospital if I had a sense of adventure.

My desire for adventure grew with each year and each trip, but each year my understanding of adventure migrated. I knew, after working with Mark, that adventure didn't primarily relate to places but to people.

The thing that really drove my desire to go to South Sudan was a desire to better understand Deng, who was a mystery to me.

I didn't only want to understand Deng, though. Shortly after getting out of the psych ward, I read Gabriel García Márquez's *Strange Pilgrims*, a book of twelve short stories about South Americans dislocated in Europe. The book had a wisdom, elegance and melancholy, and seemed to be able to say so much about two continents.

You never understand your home better than when you are away from it, and much is revealed about a society by the way it receives new arrivals from strange lands.

I loved that book and read many of its stories multiple times. When I started travelling overseas, I often became very interested in the people from those countries who now lived their lives in Australia. I came across so many stories that could be revealed with some curiosity and a few words of another language. One day, I met a kebab shop owner who had been a surgeon in Baghdad and, another day, a plasterer who had once flown F-1s for the Shah's army before Iran's Islamic revolution. On the way from the airport, having just flown back from Lebanon, I had a taxi driver who had been an Amal guerrilla. When I told him I'd been to the town where he had fought against the Israel Defense Force, he grinned and removed his wrap-around sunglasses to show me the hole where his left eye had been before shrapnel pierced it during that fight.

I first became interested in the Sudanese refugee experience while working with Mark Hunt. I often saw Sudanese people on the train as I travelled west to meet the fighter. They always stood out. Most were relative recent arrivals and that fact, alongside a distinct aesthetic and exceptionally dark skin, made them seem separate, even in Western Sydney where there's such a strong mix of people with Asian, Indian, Middle Eastern and Polynesian ethnicity.

I wanted to understand Deng Adut the individual and Deng Adut the Dinka but also what the story of his young life may say about Sydney and Australia.

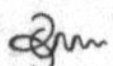

At the heart of Deng's story is his older brother, John Mac Acuek, who had been an officer in the SPLA and fled the country with his wife, Elizabeth, his baby and a teenaged Deng.

Shortly before Deng and I left for Africa, I visited Elizabeth in Blacktown and the visit reminded me of meeting Mark's sister Victoria in Auckland.

Both Elizabeth and John had struggled when they arrived in Sydney, in the relationship and in their new country. They had different expectations of what life would be like in Sydney. And while she loved Deng, he wasn't an easy teenager. He had only recently been removed from battle and the experience of being a soldier. He was highly strung and traumatised, and was harried by insomnia and bad dreams.

John worked on an undergraduate degree at Western Sydney University while teenage Deng learned English by watching *The Wiggles*. John worked on his masters at the University of Geneva as Deng went to TAFE and gained a high school equivalency. But John had trouble finding the white-collar work he wanted, something Deng credits to John just being 'too early'. He was only offered work with aid organisations that wanted him to return to East Africa and usually Sudan. But he didn't want to go back to Africa.

After years of doing unskilled work at a slaughterhouse, John relented and went back to Africa in 2005. Initially, his African return was disastrous. Heading up an Oxfam project in Sudan, John had refused a local warlord's demand to hand over his trucks and radios and was thrown in a pit where others had been killed and he was left for dead.

It took days for an Australian consulate intervention, and when John was taken from the pit, he was changed, emotionally and physically. In Sydney, he was diagnosed with a rare skin disease, developed from sitting in a puddle of faeces and blood. From then on, it was painful for his skin to be exposed to the cold.

John believed he was somehow tied to Africa, and returned to Sudan where a ceasefire was in effect. By the time South Sudan was established as an independent nation in 2011, John was a successful businessman and may have been a millionaire. Providing services in the reconstruction economy, John owned part of a number of businesses, including a hotel, a brickworks and a small airline.

John returned a couple of times a year to Sydney, where he tried to continue to be a patriarch but Elizabeth and Deng chafed against his wishes. Elizabeth was lonely and stressed and wanted John to liquidate some of his business assets to make her life easier in Sydney. All the while, Deng was furiously studying.

John saw Deng graduate from Western Sydney University before he returned to Sudan. When the South Sudanese Civil War broke out soon after, John and some other men armed themselves and rushed up a dirt road north from Juba, hoping to evacuate their families. They ran into the battlefront and John was chased, caught, shot and killed.

John's death was one of an estimated 383,000 people who died over the six-year war. All of those deaths were felt deeply somewhere. John's was felt in Western Sydney.

As I sat with Elizabeth, she told me about her frustration with John, and her anger. She told me about their divorce which, in Dinka culture, required her to travel to him in Juba and explain all the ways he'd disappointed her and vice versa in front of family. John had pleaded with her not to dissolve the marriage. I think Elizabeth and John really loved each other but she was done. The divorce went through. A year later, John was dead.

As I spoke to Elizabeth, John seemed to permeate the space between the bricks and seemed to be in the fabric of the curtains. Although the portrait of a different Sudanese man, her new husband, hung above her as she spoke, it seemed to me that John still lived in Elizabeth. Her memories were unprocessed and raw.

After a couple of hours chatting, I thanked Elizabeth and left. I went home and wondered whether that was what grief was: the refusal to have only part of the deceased person in memory, which would allow the living to be in a comfortable and convenient present. Instead there is a choice to keep the deceased person whole, and to drag with you a disordered past. It also occurred to me that if that's what grief is, then there's real beauty in that.

I came home and thought about the fact that I'd spent so much of my life denigrating and being suspicious of tradition and customs, and suspicious of earnestness, especially those people who assign importance to everything that happens to them, claiming revelation every second day.

This was a trait that had undoubtedly developed in childhood, passed down from my dad. It was balanced by a wonder and interest in the world around me, but it left me as an observer in the world more than a participant.

For a long time, I failed to understand that having earnestness in life was important, and that assigning almost spiritual significance to some moments, rituals and people was also important.

Life can be so light and so fragile sometimes, like a long ribbon of tissue paper laid out on rocky ground. It's unable to move, flow and dance if too restricted, but also too flimsy without some parts of it being weighted.

One obvious example is marriage. Weddings are an outmoded, anachronistic, patriarchal throwback and seemingly pointless in a secular environment. Yet I've loved weddings ever since my friends started marrying.

I love them as a day when we all break away from our regular lives, change our style of dress, come together and watch friends make the outlandish and very earnest statement that they will love one another forever.

I also appreciate the bravery of weddings, because marriage is one of the few chosen aspects of life that can't be easily undone. A love affair should leave a mark, but a marriage is seismic and defining, as it should be.

After interviewing Elizabeth, I thought of my mum. While eating in a little suburban trattoria in Napoli, the day after we'd been in Pompeii, my sister and I had speculated out loud about the prospect of Mum meeting someone new.

Mum shut the speculation down immediately. She told me that her marriage pledge to my dad had been a once-in-a-lifetime romantic commitment. As far as I know, she's never been in another romantic relationship.

I often wished that Mum had been open to meeting someone new, but I was also impressed by, and respectful of, her steadfast dedication to what she saw as the parameters of romantic love.

Elizabeth married again but with each movement, each word, each sigh, it was obvious that she, like my mum, believed in the weight and counterweight of commitment and love.

Days after meeting Elizabeth, Deng and I flew to Africa. I left with the feeling that I had some understanding of Elizabeth but that I was yet to really understand anything about Deng.

Juba's airport was a hot, chaotic mess when we arrived. Armed men in uniforms milled, passengers agitated, flies buzzed and Deng and I split, he to the line for those with South Sudanese passports and I to the 'others' line.

Deng had brought two outfits to Africa with him: one a jacket, shirt and waistcoat, matched with designer jeans, designer loafers or boots, a scarf, usually silk, and an RM Williams hat with a long feather in the band. The other was a black Jordan brand tracksuit with gleaming and expensive sneakers. As we went through customs, he was wearing the former, and as he spoke to the soldier who was processing his passport, I could see he and Deng were in an animated conversation. When we were reunited at baggage claim, Deng was without his hat. I asked what happened and he said he knew that soldier.

'It's okay. I owed him a hat,' Deng said.

It was the first of many interactions that helped me understand the way the city and country was managed. We were welcomed at the airport by some of Deng's family and friends and spent some days in the capital with them in cars that uniformly had rifles and handguns in the boot or on the back seat. Deng was welcome, but he was a guest like I was. There was an established way of doing things in Juba. John had known that way of doing things, but his brother, the Australian lawyer, did not.

One day, Deng was called to the compound of an SPLA general in what, it seemed to me, was an obligation. I was told to stay outside with a dozen men, some in uniform, lounging under the shade of the large veranda of a dilapidated compound surrounded by a rusty fence.

The man Deng visited was one of the architects of the child mobilisation in the 1980s; a hero of the liberation, but also the man who sent Deng into military enslavement. In a fictional story, Deng may have had a moment of confrontation and release with the general, but this story is not fictional. While I waited for Deng, one of the men told me about his feelings for any South Sudanese who left the country during the war, gained educations and now wanted to run the country. His feelings were not generous.

It became obvious that war service, even service undertaken as a child, was valued very highly in South Sudan. As was armed service for your tribe.

For me, the story I was writing was set in motion by a war that was a long time and a long way away from my life in Australia. But the war was not distant here and that had to be kept in mind for any man living here and with family here.

Later that day, Deng and I were in a busy market and a dusty black four-wheel drive shadowed us for twenty or thirty metres before pulling alongside. A window rolled down and a man called out to Deng. Deng's face lit up. This was Ajak Bior, who had also been conscripted as a child from a rural village and had built a friendship with Deng when they had both fought in the Jaish Army, as their unit was called. Ajak also fled South Sudan during the war, but stayed in East Africa. From a refugee camp, he went to Sudan's capital, Khartoum, where he earned his degree.

Ajak showed Deng and I around his impressive legal offices before driving us to a fortified camp with a bar pressed up against the White Nile River. We ordered gin and tonics and took a table close to the water.

Deng and Ajak compared their lives and their work. I was confounded by the fact that they had both become successful lawyers, as both had left the most rural villages in Africa not to go to school but to fight in a traumatising war. I told Ajak that I was confounded. He shrugged.

'In the Jaish Army, we figured out how to keep going, how to figure out how to get to the end of the day. We learned how to do what we had to. Those skills transferred I think,' Ajak said. 'And the boys who didn't have those skills are all dead.'

Deng and Ajak started comparing wounds and I went to the bar for another round of gins. The bartender, who knew Ajak, asked who I was. I told him I was writing a book with Deng. He asked what Deng's story was and I told him quickly.

'Like him?' the bartender said, pointing to Ajak with the knife he was using to cut a lemon for our drinks. The man didn't understand where the interest in the book would be and it made me begin to wonder too.

Deng and I flew north from Juba in a tiny old Cessna, following the White Nile River towards Bor, his home state. Deng grabbed my shoulder and gestured to the river below, shaking his head. I knew what he was showing me. Deng had earlier been telling me that it was an outrage that most of the deaths suffered in the recent wars had been due to either the mismanagement of water and arable lands or their deliberate use as tools of war.

Deng had been exasperated when telling me that no one in South Sudan need starve and yet the World Food Programme estimates that three-quarters of the population of South Sudan are facing food insecurity and 2 million children and women face acute malnutrition.

Deng and I landed at a tiny airport in Bor and went to the local market. Boxes of AK-47 rifles were being sold for US$20–$30 apiece and 7.62 ammunition at 50 cents a round, alongside bags of wheat, flour, dried spices, powdered milk and more. Deng bought as much of the foodstuffs as could be loaded into our van and we drove south, along the river and into the bush.

Deng's childhood village was not only a world away from Sydney, it was a world away from Juba. Two older, half-naked women stopped grinding maize when we arrived. A man in traditional dress with a spear appeared from a small hut. Children ran to us when they saw Deng and then scattered when they saw me. Deng's mum, Athieu, appeared and she bounced and vibrated and yelled and charged towards her boy.

When they embraced, it was magical. There was love, truly. Being together again was something both had dreamed about often during the war. Now it was happening. Deng and his mother didn't spend long hours together, though. There was love between the two, but not familiarity. We met long-lost family members and even half brothers and sisters, but we never spent much time in the village. The village was still close to what it had been when Deng was six. There was no power, no gas, no plumbing and the buildings were mostly made of river mud and thatch. People fished and traded and lived a traditional life. People died without modern medical intervention, like Deng's father whose grave was filled before Deng was born.

It was as unfamiliar an environment for Deng as Sydney would be for Athieu.

Deng had long dreamed of being back in his village with his mother and, when we worked on the book, he would stress over and over again how important his mother was to him. But the truth was they were almost like strangers living in different worlds. Deng was drawn to this village and his mother, but he wasn't comfortable when we were there. This is one of the tragedies of the war. An entire generation of Sudanese boys were taken to a hellish purgatory that was neither the life they'd led before, nor one they'd have in the future. They could never return to their old lives and could only go forwards with great effort and gumption.

When we left, Deng had an intense conversation with his mother, which seemed to me to be a negotiation. There was something she wanted and Deng seemed to be explaining what he could do for her.

I asked what they'd been talking about and he said his mum had asked him to marry a girl in Sydney and then bring her to South Sudan so she could live with Athieu in the village.

'Mum doesn't understand Australian women,' Deng said as we drove away.

Deng and I drove north of Bor to what looked like an abandoned village. In that village, there was a large but simple single-storey building, obviously abandoned. Next to it was another, smaller building, also abandoned. The large building had been a school and the second building was a toilet block for female students. These buildings were conceived of, built and paid for by Deng's brother, John Mac Acuek. It was a project that died with its patron.

As Deng and I poked around the school in the blistering midday sun, a woman arrived from seemingly nowhere.

She and Deng spoke for a while in Dinka and the woman took us to a mound of dirt under a large tree. Deng explained that this was John's grave.

He and I stood, staring with the Nile to the left of us, the school behind us and John in front of us. In my memory, the whole scene is blanched and white, as though shot with overexposed film. I can still hear the persistent cacophony of insects.

We stood, we stared and then Deng fell to his knees and cried. The emotion just came, through all the kinetic bluster, all the defence mechanisms, all the rest of Deng. He stayed on his knees and rubbed the mound gently with his palms. He then removed his shirt and his watch and buried them in the pile.

I'd never seen such emotion from Deng before, not even when interviewing him and talking about the most intimate details of his life. I'd not even seen anything close. I've not really seen anything since either.

Back in the van, we headed towards Bor, and Deng started talking about how much he'd appreciate a cold Tusker beer, something we couldn't get in the guesthouse we'd been staying at. I told him how deeply I, too, would appreciate a cold beer. By the time we had arrived in Bor, we'd made the perhaps foolhardy decision to keep driving south where, in five hours' time, we could be drinking a Tusker beer.

We drove on a dirt road past gunmen and roadblocks and rusted-out tanks, cattle camps and the site of John's gunfight. Once, with the light failing, we got bogged and had to contemplate the prospect of a night in the middle of the bush. The dangerous reality of the situation set in later, but in that moment, both Deng and I stripped off and slipped and slid and pushed and grunted our way out of the bog. Afterwards, we were ebullient and pretty much laughed our way to the fortified camp in Juba where we could have the first sip of an icy cold Tusker beer.

I went to bed that night thinking about the strange and wild day and of the contrast between the solemnity of finding John's grave in the morning and the giddy, dangerous rush across the country to a cold beer. I thought about how both grief and joy can also be a swift intrusion of truth into the artifice that is ourselves.

I knew even then that this was a day I'd always remember. This day had been one of unmistakable excitement with elements verging on the cinematic, but it had also been one in which I felt I'd started to understand Deng and was now ready to write his book.

Deng's complicated but deeply felt relationships with John and his mother were important. They created inertia and impetus in his life and helped him maintain his strong belief that life was important – both his own and others'.

They were significant drivers behind Deng becoming a man for whom justice isn't just a set of rules but the natural state of a perfect world, something worth striving towards every day and something that everyone in the world should have access to.

Deng loved his mother and brother above all things, but his mother was functionally a stranger to him and his brother was dead. The unfairness of that fact created energy in him, and that energy could have easily been applied to tribal animus or perhaps even greed, thinking that something material is owed to him.

The energy didn't go there, though. It went to a promise. When Deng arrived in Australia, he was told that it was a country in which every person's rights were equally applied, regardless of their ancestry, their background and the colour of their skin. A citizen of Australia who had ancestry back to Governor Phillip had the same rights as someone who was Dinka-born, SPLA-trained and recently arrived, or so the promise claimed.

Of course, in practise, that wasn't the reality that Deng found in Australia. There are many ways in which inequality perpetuates in Australia, and the primary one is access to the law. When having a dispute with a person or institution, you may have righteousness on your side but if they have lawyers and you don't then you are disadvantaged. Deng recognised this fact. So he became a lawyer himself, working primarily on immigration and minor criminal issues for people with refugee backgrounds.

Deng was never going to make access to the law equal but he was at least going to dedicate his life to making it less unequal. As a former cynic, I saw this as an act of heroism.

Songs of a War Boy was a success and its publication created a period of intense interest in Deng. The oratorial power that I experienced at the Rotary Club in Blacktown was shared across the country in print and in radio and television interviews. Deng was awarded the New South Wales Law Society President's Medal, a portrait of him won the Archibald People's Choice Prize, the book was optioned for a film and Deng was named New South Wales Australian of the Year. The bookies then had Deng as the unbackable favourite to become Australian of the Year.

But when Dr Alan Mackay-Sim, a biomedical scientist treating spinal cord injuries, was announced as the Australian of the Year, I breathed a small sigh of relief.

If Deng had become the Australian of the Year, he would have had to continue in public as just one Deng. I feared that would have been hard work and, if he slipped in that effort, he may have been attacked, likely by Australian media outlets and their penchant for the 'ungrateful refugee' narrative.

After Australia Day, Deng disappeared somewhat from the public eye. I caught up with him every few months afterwards and sometimes he was in a good place and sometimes it seemed he wasn't. Sometimes he even told me he was moving back to South Sudan, once asking me to take over his share in his law firm. I often suggested that he get some therapeutic help and it seemed he got bored with me asking if he had. To this day, I think Deng is a man straddling two continents, a man who can't quite gain a footing in either. I have to admit, I still don't fully understand Deng. Although I know what images are in his head, I'll never really know how Deng processes them.

Deng is a complex man, perhaps reflecting the complexity of the trauma he's experienced, but the fact that he still functions, still feels and still cares as he does is what makes Deng a great Australian.

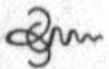

I see Deng's face every day now, on my corkboard grinning as he stands with his arm around my dad at the Octagon Theatre in Perth. Deng was in Western Australia for the Perth Writer's Festival and Dad had just moved back to

Western Australia with Marlene after their daughters started having their own daughters.

'It feels like I've found my tribe,' Dad told me once while playing with Laura's girls, who were the reason my sister went back to Western Australia also. Family craves family. Dad loved being a grandfather.

At the writer's festival, Deng told the crowd that he had lost a brother in war, but then found one while writing the book. He went further, saying he'd lost his father as a child and now his new brother's father was also his father.

These were the kinds of things Deng would say: funny but serious; outrageous, but also deeply felt.

Deng called for my dad to stand up. The house lights went up and Dad had no choice but to stand. Deng then called for the audience to give my dad a round of applause, which they did enthusiastically.

Even now, the idea of that moment makes me laugh. Dad would have squirmed in his Rivers shoes as he felt the eyes of an audience on him, and the round of applause would have taken him out of his body.

The photograph taken afterwards is a favourite of mine, because of Deng's wild, happy grin, but also because of the look on Dad's face. For most people, Dad's expression would have been indecipherable but I know what the slight rising of his eyebrows, the catching of his cheeks and the relaxed lips mean. I can tell that in the photo, Dad was happy, and happy because he's proud.

If you asked me whether I became a writer to impress my dad, I would have said no. I would have told you that I was a rugged individualist, carving a path that is mine and mine alone. If you had asked my dad if he hoped that I would work as a writer, a vocation he respected greatly, he probably would have said no too.

Neither answer would have been true, even though both Dad and I would have believed what we said.

When working with Deng, I thought often about how unseen forces move our lives, both his and mine.

I think family craves family at least in part because, consciously or not, humans crave a place in a continuum. We are all our parents' children and they their parents' children. We are all people in a family, a community, born of a country. When we are denied a spot in family, community or country, we can yearn to be reconnected, we can agitate and we can also suffer.

This is something I considered when working with Deng, and when working later with the great chronicler of the Stolen Generations, Archie Roach, and when thinking about my dad's life.

Chapter 11

on addiction, on archie roach

Songs of a War Boy would not be the last book I'd write about the effects of trauma. In fact, trauma would become a theme in my work and I would learn a great deal about the phenomenon.

One thing I learned early on is that trauma can be contagious. I learned it through literature, reading that partners of Australia's Vietnam veterans were six times more likely to take their own lives than the rest of the Australian population and that the children of holocaust survivors are more likely to express a gene related to stress and PTSD than a control group. I learned it through experience also.

When working with Mark, I had intrusive feelings and thoughts of the house he grew up in; when working with Deng I had a full false flashback of the battle in which he was blown up and shot.

While intrusive, these feelings and thoughts never became unmanageable. They arrived, were used and then disappeared when I sent my manuscript off for editing. I credit that fact to Bondi.

Bondi was the place where I washed the residue of interviews off me. Bondi was the land that trauma forgot. They say that sunshine is a disinfectant, and I say sea-spray is therapy and it was therapy I'd been utilising well before I started writing books.

When I had my stroke, I was still living close to the city but it was then that I started regularly going to Bondi. By the time I had my heart attack, I was living in a shared apartment a short walk from the beach and I found it to be the perfect place to recover.

When I was panicked, doubting or depressed, being close to the ocean was calming, and there was something about the atmosphere of Bondi that made me want to walk, even at a time when it was tiring to do.

I still love to walk around Bondi, usually hoping to bump into the community of beach volleyballers and their friends and family that I've built up over the decade spent in the suburb.

Unlike the Cottesloe beach volleyball community I found of highly skilled players, mostly athletic young men and almost all Australian born, the community in Bondi was different. It was multilingual, multi-gendered, European, north and south American, African and Australian and spread all across the socio-economic spectrum. The community is stronger because of it.

We are all very different people, but we have one common trait and that trait is that we all chose Bondi as a place where we can live our lives happily and slowly.

People in Bondi owned multi-million-dollar houses, drove European cars and ate at Bill Granger's restaurant. But that was a different Bondi. Our Bondi was a long strip of sand, sunny days on the beach playing volleyball, rainy days at the Gertrude & Alice bookstore café drinking coffee, tap beer at The Royal pub and overpopulated barbecues in undersized rented apartments.

I think living in Bondi hastened my physical and emotional recovery from my heart attack and the surgeries that followed. I also think that, with its cliffs to read on, ocean for swimming in, beach to play volleyball on and dozens of familiar faces, Bondi has been the perfect counterweight to the heaviness of the subject matter I've chosen to write about. It has kept away the demons that many of the subjects of my books have been hounded by.

While I was working on this book, I listened to Mark Hunt on a podcast, talking about the process of writing *Born to Fight*, and during the interview he jokingly mentioned that he'd gambled heavily in Auckland while we were doing those first interview sessions. When pressed, Mark said he lost a few hundred thousand dollars during that time. It was disheartening to hear but not surprising. Mark admitted that he'd suffered a life-long addiction to poker-machine gambling, although he had migrated it into a relatively benign obsession with video games.

The relationship between trauma and addiction is well established. More than half of those diagnosed with PTSD also having diagnosable addiction issues, and many of the neurological changes seen in people who are experiencing trauma are in line with neurological abnormalities seen in long-term addicts.

The human brain evolved in community and is built to exist and to operate in a community. Sufferers of trauma may be physically close to people – their family, their colleagues, their neighbours – but if they can't connect with these people they are isolated. Studies have suggested that isolation may breed isolation in a vicious cycle. Mice studies show that isolated subjects develop smaller hippocampi and amygdalae. A constricted hippocampus is linked to impaired learning and memory, and a constricted amygdala limits the sufferer's capacity for emotional processing and social understanding. This change 'compromises neural structure and function, rendering an individual susceptible to ... substance abuse'.

It seems that trauma establishes yearnings that are fed by addiction, usually to the great detriment of the sufferer.

One of the yearnings is for opioids – substances that can act on receptors in the brain, creating a feeling of contentedness and well-being. A healthy person's opioids are created naturally in the body. As part of the opioid attachment-reward system, they are generated when creating or maintaining social bonds and affiliation, especially with family.

This can be difficult for a trauma sufferer and, with the loss of naturally occurring opioids, they may be more susceptible to the abuse of and addiction for substances that may have similar effect, which can be synthetic opioids, but could also be booze, heroin or even marijuana.

Another yearning trauma sufferers may have is for dopamine, a neurotransmitter that is part of an incentive and motivation reward system in the brain. Dopamine release creates a feeling of pleasure, satisfaction and motivation in the brain, gently rising after new experiences or exercise, then slowly receding in a balanced and joyful way. Trauma can affect this system, especially in those who suffer trauma as a child, sometimes creating a surplus of dopamine, which can make the sufferer more competitive and aggressive and demonstrate poor impulse control, or a deficit that can have a dangerous deadening effect.

In both instances, the sufferer will be more susceptible to activities that release a dopamine hit, which may include online shopping, posting on social media and gambling. Especially gambling.

Charles Livingstone, an associate professor at the School of Public Health and Preventive Medicine at Monash University, found that poker machines are an especially dangerous form of gambling for people who have suffered trauma, primarily because the machines are designed to hack our dopamine-reward system. It has also been found that the machines are designed to put the user in a dopamine 'flow state', in which time is distorted, dopamine is maximised and the gambling goes on for hours (or, in the case of Mark Hunt after winning his first major tournament, three days).

After the brain has unnaturally been bombarded with dopamine, it takes some time for the brain's dopamine incentive and motivation reward systems to return to their normal state in healthy people. It takes even longer for those who are experiencing trauma, and this is one of the reasons they are so susceptible to addiction.

Poker machines are found in casinos all over the world, but most of the poker machines in the world (seventy-five per cent) that are found outside casinos are in Australia, usually concentrated in areas where levels of trauma are highest: in areas of economic depression; venues where military veterans are likely to attend, especially Returned and Services League Clubs; and places where First Nations people live and gather.

Ruby Hunter was addicted to poker machines. When ghost-writing a book with her husband, Archie Roach, who, like Ruby, was a notable Indigenous musician and community activist, I witnessed that nothing riled him up like poker machines. 'Those bloody things,' the mild-mannered Archie would call the machines that drained his wife of her time, and their family its savings.

Ruby didn't see her use of the machines as an addiction, though. Mostly because it didn't seem like one when scaled against the epic alcohol addiction that both she and Archie suffered, and that nearly killed him.

When Ruby and Archie met at a halfway house in Adelaide as teens, they already had alcohol abuse in common, as well as a shared history of trauma and disconnection. Both had been taken from their families when they were children, as part of the Stolen Generations. Their story was a shared journey from disconnection and addiction to connection, sobriety and love.

Archie started drinking pretty much as soon as a letter from a sister he didn't know he had arrived at his school, telling him of the passing of his mother, someone he'd believed had died in a house fire when he was a baby. The letter also spoke of other siblings he didn't know he had, scattered around the state and country.

Archie was a good student in a safe house with loving foster parents, yet he was compelled to hit the road after the letter arrived. He wanted to find his family and his culture, which he knew nothing about.

Archie quickly fell in with 'the parkies' as he called the homeless Aboriginal people who congregated and sometimes resided in public places. On the road, he also found his family. Both offered him the stories he yearned for.

Archie learned about the Gunditjmara, his mother's people, and the Bundjalung, his father's people. He learned about their land and their lives and about the mission where he was born. He heard his parents' stories and their language, he also heard the stories of his brothers and sisters, as well as those of his uncles, aunties, cousins and nephews, which were also his stories.

Many of the stories he heard were devastating: of a culture deliberately atomised, ancestors killed and of a family separated by a state that didn't allow him or his ancestors voting rights.

Archie drank with his family, and with the parkies. He said he did so to allow them all to be together; something they all really wanted but something that was so painful it reminded each of them of all the death and dispossession.

Ruby, who had also been a drinker, cleaned up successfully after the birth of their second child. Ruby tried to get Archie to clean up. And when he couldn't, she left him.

He then went on a 'die-or-quit' bender. This resulted in Archie suffering a 'generalised tonic-clonic seizure', formerly known as a 'grand mal seizure', in which the chemical neurotransmitters in the brain are imbalanced, creating a surge of electrical activity that engages parts of the brain in an unwanted way.

After the seizure, Archie woke in hospital suffering through his last ever hangover. He realised then that he could keep drinking and die alone, or stop and live with Ruby and the kids.

It was a desire for connection that had pushed Archie to drink, and it was also a desire for connection that inspired him to stop. Connection was also a tool in his recovery.

Ruby and Archie reconnected and Archie joined Alcoholics Anonymous, a twelve-step program that Archie credits his sobriety to.

While in recovery, Archie found a way in which he and other Indigenous people could soberly but happily connect and share stories. Archie had always played the guitar, but it was only after sobering up that he started to write songs, most of which were biographical.

He sang songs about drinking and sobering up, and about his life on the road. Initially he sang to small, mostly Aboriginal audiences, often other recovering addicts, until 26 January 1988, 200 years since the arrival of the First Fleet.

That day, Archie, Ruby and their kids had joined a large group protesting the lack of recognition of the pain that had been felt by First Nations Australians over the last two centuries. They marched through Sydney, ending at a camp in La Perouse, at the mouth of Botany Bay, where a PA system had been set up and protestors were welcomed to tell their stories.

Archie went up with his acoustic guitar and played 'Took the Children Away', a song that became an anthem for the Stolen Generations. It's a song that starts with pain and ends with a flourish of hope, singing about the day that all the children will come back, to country and to family.

When Australian singer and songwriter Paul Kelly saw Archie play the song later that year, he invited Archie to support him at a gig in Melbourne. After a devastating and brilliant performance, Kelly visited Archie and Ruby's house and offered to produce an album for Archie.

The album became *Charcoal Lane*, named after a famous parkies' spot in Fitzroy, and spawned two successful singles: 'Took the Children Away' and another song about their homeless years called 'Down City Streets', written by Ruby, who had been learning guitar after Archie cleaned up.

So began not one ground-breaking musical career, but two. Archie became an ARIA Hall of Fame musician and Ruby became the first Indigenous woman signed to a major Australian label.

In 2010, Ruby Hunter died suddenly. One moment, she was playing Nintendo with her grandkids and the next she had suffered a heart attack that instantly killed her.

Ruby and Archie had been two parts of a whole and, with Ruby's absence, addiction returned to Archie's life. Not booze this time but marijuana. Archie smoked into a state of near catatonia. It is a time he remembers little of, but he does remember its end.

Archie stared at himself in the mirror, stricken and unkempt. In this moment, his unconscious mind conjoined with Ruby. When Archie told me about this, he described Ruby as though she was there. She looked at him in the mirror and was disappointed. She asked him how he thought he looked. Archie stared at his whiskers and bloodshot eyes framed by deep bags.

'Not good, Mum,' he replied.

For years, Archie had called her Mum and she had called him Dad. Ruby told him that he'd wallowed enough. It was time to have a shave, stop smoking weed and get back into his work.

Archie told me that she'd said the same thing to him then that she'd said to him when Paul Kelly had left their house for the first time and Archie had told her he didn't think he wanted to make an album.

'It's not all about you, Archie Roach.'

Ruby told Archie she just wanted one thing, to go back to the river and her country, and afterwards he should go back to work.

Ruby had been born on the banks of an island on the Murray River in South Australia and had lived with the Ngarrindjeri, Kokatha and Pitjantjatjara people until, at age eight, she too was taken from her family and sent into foster care. Throughout her life, Ruby had maintained a very strong spiritual connection to the river and the Coorong.

Archie took Ruby's remains back to her country and, after a service, planned to go back to work. Time caught up with Archie, though. Time and the hardness of his life. Archie suffered a stroke, and for a time couldn't play the guitar, and then he was also diagnosed with lung cancer.

Archie told me the possibility of performing again and the possibility of writing again were the things that kept him going. And perform and write he did.

Before Ruby died, Archie had written the song 'Mulyawongk', a tribute to Ruby and the spirit of the river who called for her to come back. He reworked and recorded it after his recovery in the wake of her death. In 2012, the song was included in what is my favourite of Archie's albums, *Into the Bloodstream*.

I started working with Archie in 2018, when he was near the end of his life. He was largely wheelchair-bound by then and during one of the first times I was with Archie he suffered an attack of the chronic obstructive pulmonary disease that took his life.

We were beside the stage at the Palais Theatre in St Kilda, where he was set to perform, when the attack came on. After trying to walk up a small incline to the stage, Archie started to choke, gulping air as best he could but the yield to his lungs was too meagre. Archie often travelled with an oxygen bottle but, in this instance, it had been left in his hotel room perhaps six or seven hundred metres away.

I ran as fast as I could to his room and brought back the bottle. Archie was slumped in his chair but conscious. He breathed in and out from the oxygen bottle and, after a minute or two, he asked me to help him to a chair on stage. With the hubbub of the crowd able to be heard through the thick curtain, Archie gulped deeply from the oxygen mask before asking for the bottle to be taken away and his guitar to be handed to him.

Archie played, as he always did, magically, with his eyes often closed, his hands reaching out as he conjured an unmistakable Australian spirit. When the applause subsided and the curtain fell, Archie crumpled back into his wheelchair.

The next day, I interviewed Archie and we spoke about the day Ruby died. The interview ended with both of us in tears. That night, we attended an event hosted by Corrections Victoria, where Archie was going to perform and talk about efforts he and his friend Jack Charles had been undertaking for the last few years. The pair would visit youth correctional facilities, perform, meet the inmates and then connect with Indigenous youth who didn't know about their families or mob, and try to connect them to their history and their people. Both Uncle Archie and Uncle Jack deeply believed that isolation from culture and continuum was something that fostered pain, addiction and the conditions for criminality.

The next day, we went back to Archie's house in his country, which was close to Port Fairy in south-west Victoria. At his kitchen table, we kept working. Archie's work ethic was inspiring. He was driven to tell his story, write his music and perform, and yet none of the drive came from a place of ego. It all came from a simple desire to tell a story and, if he could, make a difference. While working with Archie, I often thought that his drive came from the respect he had for life itself. When he'd describe even the simplest of life's pleasure, like Cottee's cordial in very cold water, he did so with an infectious sense of joy.

I left Archie's and drove east to Adelaide where Mark Hunt was to have his last UFC fight. On the way, I drove through Murray Bridge, a town that Archie and Ruby had lived in, and I pulled up at a park overlooking the Murray. It was a grey day and I played *Into the Bloodstream* on the stereo as a dark, flat, fast river rushed in front of me. When I listened to 'Mulyawongk', I felt myself filled up, probably with endogenic dopamine and opioids. I felt sadness, but more than that, I felt waves of gratitude: for this world, this country and this vocation that I'd found.

An important link between Australia's past and present was severed in July 2022 at Warrnambool Base Hospital, when Archie Roach left us. An important link between the past and present survives in the movies and television series that Uncle Archie contributed to, in his book *Tell Me Why*, and, most essentially, in his music.

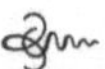

The opportunity to work in the way I did with Archie – and with Mark Hunt, Deng Adut and others – didn't afford me much in the way of money or recognition, yet I considered it a privilege.

It allowed me to sit at the counter of an East African coffee roasters, in the corner of a New Zealand fighting gym, on a bench at an Aboriginal nature reserve and ask a person whose life is exceptional: 'Who *are* you?'

In their answers, I learned a lot about trauma, ego and pride. I learned a lot about men. I spent a lot of time talking about the nuance and boundaries of morality with people who'd seen those edges. I learned a lot about Australia also. I discovered attitudes and perspectives that couldn't be seen from the comfortable middle of Australian life.

Without the conversations, experiences and ruminations those co-authored books afforded, I would have found it hard to understand the extremity of experience I discovered when I started working with veterans of Australia's special forces wars in Afghanistan and Iraq.

The co-authored books also allowed me to write hundreds of thousands of words about love and hate and life's contemplations; themes I'd never have written about in my own voice.

I'd wanted to write and publish since I'd watched *The Killing Fields* as a teenager, and I did, but for so long I did it with half of my heart. Until I had my stroke and heart attack.

Writing became harder after those medical events, but also easier. Harder because the technical aspects of the craft were sometimes not easy. I had brain damage. I have brain damage. I can feel it now, writing as I am at the end of the day, where words start to flutter around and tenses swap themselves.

Easier because the fear of writing earnestly started to leave. I started to realise that the penny of doubt or embarrassment is just a penny. It helped that I was writing in someone else's voice, but it was only in my thirties that I was able to write with passion, in one book and the next and the next.

The removal of those self-imposed shackles was a gift given to me by traumatic events. Those events also introduced me to the concept of enough.

After my stroke and heart attack, I had conceived the possibility of an abruptly short life, and when it seemed that life would go on, my perspective changed. I didn't see my life in blocks of years or decades, but days.

A good day was some writing, some exercise, a swim, a book or a film, food, friends and a beer or two. Perhaps a date, sometimes with people who I was with for weeks or months, but usually with women who had little desire for their lives to change significantly either. Every couple of months, I'd be off to Perth or overseas for some adventure or another.

I sometimes wonder whether I would actually have been happy living that life into my forties and on to my fifties and sixties. I think it's possible, primarily because of that concept of enough and one other factor: I had learned how to manage loneliness.

After the split with my long-time girlfriend, I spent a lot of time alone. I was someone who had historically really felt the loneliness in my life and I felt it deeply in the wake of that break-up. That period of intermittent loneliness was unique in my life, though. It came at a time when I was living a good and full life, one that just happened to have downtime.

I did some of the things that a lot of people do to assuage loneliness. I drank more than I should and had some affairs that shouldn't have started, as well as others that should have ended earlier. That period of excesses didn't last long, though, because I didn't want my life to change.

I was living an essentially happy and gratifying life, and had found work I really wanted to do. Best of all, loneliness hadn't been an entrée to the depression and mania I sometimes suffered, as I'd feared.

I didn't want to be hungover all the time, nor did I want to be in a relationship like the one I'd been in before. After a short period of drinking and dating, I decided I'd rather be lonely. I didn't need more than the people I was writing about, my friends and my family on the other side of the continent.

The more time I spent lonely, the easier it was to be lonely. That hollow feeling never went away, but after a while, I no longer felt its discomfort.

Hollowness just became part of life. The tax I paid so I could live exactly as I wanted to.

I considered my ability to manage loneliness a gift, and it was, allowing me to concentrate my life's efforts towards reading and writing. From where I am now, having been plucked out of that life and into a different one, I see that such an ability can also be a curse.

Part III

Chapter 12

happiness is a warm gun

Before I write about when and how I started writing my trilogy of books about Australia's special forces, I want to explain the circumstances around how and why I decided to stop.

It was a cold morning in June 2021 in Sydney. I'd dusted off one of my *Sport&Style* suits, caught the train to the CBD and trudged my way to the Federal Court of Australia. In front of the courthouse, I was drinking black coffee chatting with a photographer friend when she and a few dozen other journalists, camera people and photographers sprang into action and ran down Phillip Street and towards a large man wearing a dark suit.

I moved away from the commotion, through security to the lift that would take me to a courtroom on the sixteenth floor. I entered the empty lift alone, pressed the button and waited. The doors started to close until a large hand and an expensive watch intruded. Ben Roberts-Smith followed.

He was to be the first of dozens of witnesses called in a blockbuster defamation trial that Roberts-Smith was bringing against the publishers of the *Sydney Morning Herald* and *The Age* newspapers, who had accused him of being a war criminal and a domestic abuser.

Earlier in the week, both Nine Media's and Roberts-Smith's barristers had presented their cases. Nine's case had painted Roberts-Smith as a cruel killer and someone who assumed influence beyond his rank, abused that influence, dehumanised Afghans, misunderstood the war, bullied, brutalised and killed well beyond the bounds of any strategic purpose.

Roberts-Smith's blue-ribbon legal team presented him as a hard-charging and brave soldier who fought a brutal war in the manner he'd been trained to do so, and in the way that had been expected of him by his regiment and his command.

It seemed that there was no possibility that both realities could exist, but I knew they could.

As Roberts-Smith prepared to give evidence, I knew Australia's war in Afghanistan was not what it had been presented as. Not by the government and Defence, not in the hagiographic and nationalistic reporting of outlets like Seven Media, whose owner Kerry Stokes was funding Roberts-Smith's legal action, nor in some of the Nine Media and ABC reporting, who leaned heavily on the idea that some 'bad apple' NCOs had ruined Australia's reputation in a difficult but just war.

I was of the opinion that any Australian soldier who, deliberately and in cold blood, executed Afghans should be prosecuted and locked up. I was also of the opinion that the culpability of such murders should probably be shared by many in Canberra, Sydney and Perth and it hadn't been.

Almost all of the weight of Australia's part in the war's misery had been laid on the shoulders of the people who had Afghan dust in the treads of their boots. Them and their families. It was a burden felt by many people who were both perpetrator and victim of violence. It was felt by

Afghans too, by the thousands. By the tens of thousands. So many deaths. So many broken promises.

As the lift slowed, Roberts-Smith took a deep breath and seemed to steel himself for what lay ahead. The doors opened.

'Good luck,' I said. This to a man I thought to be a murderer and war criminal.

'Cheers,' he replied.

I walked towards the courtroom, wondering what I wanted from the weeks that I was about to spend in court. What testimony would feel satisfactory? And what outcome?

I'd started pulling a thread in 2015 that led me here, to this testimony, this case. I was compelled to be in this courtroom and hear this testimony. Yet I knew that at the end of this case, all that would be on offer were more threads, more questions, more disquiet.

After being in Compton, I wrote a piece about the glamour of arm's-length violence, hoping to one day write about the systems and human impact behind violence. Now I was doing that, not looking at crime in Los Angeles but war in Afghanistan. The systems involved and trauma that was left behind were complex, though. And questions of culpability, legal and moral, even more so.

When I interviewed people about the war, it often seemed that they really wanted me to feel what they felt and think what they thought. It also seemed they didn't quite know what they felt or what they thought.

I often walked away from those interviews feeling that my subject would be tortured by thoughts of that war for the rest of their life.

As I walked into court with the man most identified with the difficulties of the war, it occurred to me I was compelled to find my own feelings and thoughts about the war. Why was I so arrogant to assume I would find them?

If it had still just been me in Bondi, with my volleyball and my books and managed loneliness, I'd probably keep going and write more about Afghanistan. There would almost certainly be murder trials to come, and the trial of David McBride, the special forces whistleblower who moved to Bondi and had become an acquaintance. Perhaps there may be that Royal Commission one day. There was a lot more work to do and a lot more to discover.

It could be done by someone else. It was soon time to walk away. My life had changed and was changing.

As I walked into court, I decided that the book I was working on then, and this trial, would be enough for me.

I had been haunted by the war I barely visited. I still had the privilege of choosing to be so affected. The book I was working on would be my last about Australia's special forces and the post-9/11 wars.

In 2013, Special Air Service Regiment (SASR) trooper and Victoria Cross recipient Mark Donaldson published a memoir, *The Crossroad*. The book offered the public their first real peek into the work being done by Australia's special forces in the post-9/11 wars, and it became a surprise bestseller. In 2015, Australian publishers were offered the possibility of a similar book: the biography of Cameron Baird, VC, MG.

Like Donaldson, Baird had been a veteran of Australia's special forces. Like Donaldson, he had fought bravely in Afghanistan and had been awarded the Victoria Cross, Australia's highest military honour. Unlike Donaldson, Baird had not survived the engagement that earned him his VC, becoming the last Australian soldier to die in combat in Afghanistan. With his posthumous award, Baird became the second most decorated soldier in modern Australian history (after Ben Roberts-Smith) and a legend in Australian military circles, especially at his regiment, the 2nd Commando

Regiment which, alongside the SASR, was the gunfighting force behind Australia's Special Operations Command.

In a conference room overlooking Sydney Harbour, I met Cameron Baird's generous and kind but still devastated parents, Doug and Kaye. Doug Baird was in his sixties, tall and fit, and looking very much like the ex-Carlton footballer that he was. He told me that there was still so much he didn't know about his son's soldiering life.

Doug met me with a handshake that was as strong as you would expect, but also revealed a softness. He told me he wanted me to find out what I could about what his son had done in Afghanistan and put it in the book. I told him I'd do the best I could.

I walked away excited and yet daunted by the project. I knew only a little about the war in Afghanistan and about the role of Australia's special forces; not even enough to know that I didn't know anything at all.

My first experience with Australia's special forces soldiers was when, as a *Ralph* staffer, I undertook the special forces barrier test in 2006, after recovering from my stroke but before my heart attack. Over twenty or so hours, I swam, ran, jumped, weaved, trudged, sweated and bled while SASR and commando veterans quietly but forcefully reminded me and the other candidates that we could fuck off home and put our feet up any time we liked.

I pushed myself hard to complete the course, passing all of the tests except a 2.4-kilometre run in webbing, rifle and ammunition. That test was done in the middle of a 38-degree day, and the three of us who had completed everything else fell short by less than thirty seconds. We were given the option of repeating the 2.4-kilometre test after finishing the 15-kilometre trudge in battle gear and pack.

Even though my feet were bleeding, my body screaming and it meant nothing to me except bragging rights, I seriously considered re-running that test in the cool morning air.

I chose not to because I was going to Wales the next day to go mountain biking, courtesy of a *Ralph* advertiser and didn't want to ruin my feet further. But as I returned to Sydney later, I did muse about the lengths young men would go to put themselves just a little higher in a hierarchical system.

My second experience was when, again as a *Ralph* staffer, I was invited to participate in a large, on-base exercise run by the Incident Response Regiment (now the Special Operations Engineering Regiment) which had me being exposed to CS gas and then playing the role of a civilian involved in a chemical weapons attack (a role that surprisingly had all my clothes sheared away by giant scissors held by operators in mission-orientated protective posture suits as dozens of observers, officers, politicians, nurses and one photographer dispassionately observed).

Afterwards, I had a few more interactions with the special forces, a few interviews with veterans, some chats in a social environment and the night in Iraq when I had been protected by them. None of those experiences prepared me for the interviews I did with the soldiers who fought alongside Cameron Baird.

For the book, I interviewed about two dozen serving and retired commandos and officers. Six initial interviews happened on one long day at Sydney's Holsworthy Barracks, the home of Australia's full-time commando regiment.

I started that day being given a tour of the barracks by a very chatty and personable sergeant who had been in the same platoon as Cameron Baird in Afghanistan. He told me stories about Cameron, in Sydney, on the base in Tarin Kowt and out in gunfights. When he dropped me off at the mess, he told me something I think he'd been planning to tell me since he first heard I was coming.

'It was the time of my life,' he said of Afghanistan. 'For all of us.'

It wasn't said solemnly nor exultantly. It was just said.

At the sergeant's mess, another soldier who'd been close to Baird told me more stories about him. Then he told me his own story, about a battle he'd been involved in, in which he had killed women and children, legally, as they'd been ferrying mortars and ammunition to Afghan fighters. I could tell those killings weighed heavily on the man, and would forever, but then he said, 'I'd do it again without thinking about it.'

I spent most of that afternoon conducting a long interview with two sergeants and a corporal: men closest to Baird, one of whom had been shot the day Baird was killed. These men knew Cameron well and they were ready to talk about him in the way a biographer dreams of.

These soldiers didn't exhibit an otherworldly reverence when talking about their comrade, the way some civilians do when talking about Victoria Cross winners. They didn't outwardly express sadness when talking about him either. They just told me who Cameron had been: an excellent soldier but also a man of choices, doubt and fallibility, as we all are.

When I was leaving, the soldier who had been shot pointed to my cardiac scar, which could be seen above the buttons of my shirt, and told me his father was having heart surgery that day.

'It's odd. I just don't feel anything,' the soldier said of the surgery. 'I know I should feel anxious or sad or something, but I don't feel anything.'

Half of the men had been shot, all had killed Afghans. Some had seen friends die or be horribly injured. Some had treated those wounds, those friends.

I left Holsworthy Barracks thinking that the violence of the war in Afghanistan had far exceeded what I'd understood it to be. I also thought, although far from being qualified to make such a judgement, that almost every veteran I interviewed that day seemed to be suffering from some manner of post-combat mental health malady.

This thought was strengthened over the next few months as I spoke to many veterans who had transitioned into civilian life. These men included a veteran who shook visibly as we talked about gunfights, another who I met in a pub and who turned around to check the door behind him perhaps two dozen times as we spoke, and another who told me 'basically everyone' with his deployment history to Afghanistan was suffering the way he was and, in asking for a PTSD diagnosis, broke unofficial Special Operations Command PTSD policy of 'don't ask, don't tell'.

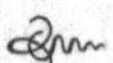

One of the men I interviewed, who didn't have any apparent post-combat issues, was one of Cameron Baird's former regimental sergeant majors. I met him at his family home in Sydney's east. This man was undoubtedly tough but also very personable and an excellent communicator. As I was leaving his house, we talked about the nature and tempo of Australia's fight in Afghanistan and how poorly it was understood by the public.

'Do you want to know how many people we killed? Us and Perth?' he asked me in his doorway, speaking of his commando regiment and the Special Air Service Regiment based in Western Australia.

'Go on.'

'Eleven thousand.'

He said it with a little laugh, dusted neither with humour nor disgust, just a residue of surprise. I left his house stunned. I knew each Australian special forces task group was only a few hundred men and women, and only a fraction of those were 'shooters' or operators like Baird.

The amount of violence each shooter would have been exposed to and would have instigated must have been immense.

That number reframed my limited understanding of the place where the Australians were fighting. I knew Uruzgan, where Australia's forces primarily operated, was a violent place (sometimes derisively described by Afghans as 'the Afghanistan of Afghanistan'). Uruzgan was a tiny province roughly the size of Australia's ACT, and only three per cent of the population of Afghanistan lived there.

In 2010, the Taliban was estimated to have 10,000 fighters in the whole country, and even a 2014 reassessment by a British general suggesting there were 25,000 to 36,000 armed insurgents, Taliban and otherwise, didn't accommodate the number that I'd been told by Baird's sergeant major.

My mind spun: who were these 11,000 people killed? And how had all this violence happened without any of us, the Australian public or the Australian media, even noticing?

In the immediate aftermath of the interview, I was only calmed by the fact that my job wasn't to wrap my arms all the way around Australia's war, nor to make any sense of this huge number. My job was to make sense of Cameron Baird's service and his life.

I maintained contact with a number of veterans I'd interviewed for the book, and one was a likeable sergeant who had been one of Baird's closest mates. This soldier was known by his peers as solidly 'staunch' – one of the great compliments that could be given in the cohort – and a 'war dog' and a 'mad cunt', further compliments.

He had found me on Facebook after I interviewed him and we chatted. One day, he messaged me and told me that he was in hospital, where he was being treated with PTSD and alcohol dependency.

'Chasing the action too long,' he told me.

His action had involved multiple tours of Afghanistan. It had also included operations in Iraq, as a private contractor and then also as a commando, and recently on a shadowy deployment in the fight against Islamic State. I wished him well and went back to writing.

I didn't hear from this soldier again, nor about him, until I'd almost finished the book. I fulfilled my promise to Doug Baird as best I could, writing truth where I found it. Cameron Baird was a good man, and a superb soldier who truly loved his job, and had no significant compunction with the killing or danger it entailed. That was Cameron Baird's story.

A couple of weeks away from deadline, a vet named Eddie, one of Cameron Baird's best friends, messaged me telling me that the soldier I had chatted to while he was in hospital had just taken his own life.

Cameron Baird didn't suffer from PTSD and yet it now seemed grotesque to ignore the magnitude of the obvious trauma revealed in many of my interview subjects. I decided to include an inscription on the first page of the book honouring those men who had been affected.

Chapter 13

externalities

I never planned to write another book about Australia's special forces, nor did I especially want to. Writing *The Commando: The life and death of Cameron Baird, VC, MG* had affected me in a way I found uncomfortable. Some of the miseries of that book lingered in me long after the launch had come and gone.

In the way that after the Gulf War I dreamed of boys being buried alive by tanks and like when working with Deng I saw the battle in which he'd been wounded, I saw, usually in the quiet of night, imagined echoes of the war in Afghanistan.

Sometimes I saw myself lying in a poppy field, dying of gunshot wounds as Australian helicopters flew away. In that vision, there was always the type of quiet that can only be felt after a great noise had ended. There's always parching thirst, too. Sometimes I saw the debilitating misery of a suicidal moment. In that moment, there's always familiar, agonising mania.

Sometimes I wondered whether my book about Cameron Baird had been a public good.

What had happened in Afghanistan had been a calamity, for Afghans and so many Australians, and while Cameron Baird's story had the shape of a classic tragedy, with the premature death of the subject assured on page one, the book itself was exhilarating. War can be exhilarating for those prosecuting it and in much of the media around it. The book was also imbued with a spirit of excitement and heroism, something Cameron Baird, as a fearless and selfless solider, earned.

There were other stories to be told, though. While working on *The Commando*, I had heard about the strategic malaise and incompetence of Defence, about our partnership with murderous warlords, about the endless hunting of spectral figures that may be key Taliban members or might just be farmers.

I also heard about war crimes: some inadvertently revealed in stories with another focus and others that were simply murders.

I knew the war in Afghanistan wasn't what it had been previously reported to be and what had been characterised by governments led by Howard to Abbott. I believed that the dissonance between what was believed about Australia's war and what was real helped create a massive burden on the men and women who were tasked with prosecuting the war. That fact bothered me and stayed with me, especially because I maintained friendships with some of the soldiers that I'd interviewed.

Then one day, a woman called me wanting to talk about her husband. She was the wife of the sergeant who had taken his own life.

She knew I'd been in conversation with him while he was in hospital and she wanted to know more. They'd become estranged towards the end of his life, and she wanted to put all the pieces together. I told her what I could, and then I asked if I could ask some questions of her also.

She was also in the military, working as a psychologist at Special Operations Command (SOCOMD). She'd trained as a psychologist after seeing how each of her husband's combat deployments sent him further and further into a mental health spiral. She told me that, while command perhaps didn't know the full extent of what her husband's mental health issues were, his officers knew that he was suffering extensively from PTSD, and that he was an alcoholic. She said they kept deploying him knowing that fact. With each deployment, his suffering worsened.

This brave woman approached her husband's commanding officer and the SOCOMD padre. She told me they were understanding to her face, but did nothing. Within the unit, it was suggested that unhappiness in their marriage was why her husband was suffering and why he was drinking.

Eventually her husband had been deemed medically unfit by Joint Health Command after a significant mental health breakdown, but he was offered a health waiver by a commanding officer. Such waivers meant that any order outside the soldier's SOCOMD chain of command could be countermanded by the flick of a commander's pen.

I had heard that the SOCOMD commanders' pens flicked often when the mental health bill from Afghanistan came due, and that men with serious mental health issues were deploying so the command could maintain battle strength.

This man had taken his own life after he'd been hospitalised for PTSD, then sent to Iraq where the Australian special forces were trying to help root Islamic State out of a number of cities that Islamic State had occupied.

I wondered a lot about that deployment. Again, almost no information about the Australian special forces role in Iraq had leaked, but I imagined what the Australian forces had done. Prime Minister Tony Abbott had made assurances to the media and public that Australia's soldiers were not directly involved in the fighting against Islamic State, but I suspected that may not have been true.

My suspicion was strengthened by a soldier I met who was in the process from retiring from the Defence Force. His career had him working as a spy at the Australian Signals Directorate and at Special Operations Command where he became beret qualified as a 'shooter', meaning he'd done all the training an operator did, but he was also qualified as an Electronic Warfare Operator (EWO). As an EWO, he would deploy into a war zone with special forces teams and intercept information from (and sometimes insert information to) enemy phones, radios and computers.

The EWO would also often be tasked with identifying and locating people, sometimes marking them for death. This was something he did in the western deserts of Iraq in 2014, on a base that was surrounded by ISIS and often attacked by ISIS. He also worked in Mosul, a modern city the size of Perth, that was occupied by ISIS and decorated with the black flags of *shahada* and bodies. There, Australians were attacked with drones, car bombs and chemical weapons.

The force attacking the Australian soldiers included Australian citizens, men from a cohort of between 250 and 300 Australians who had gone to the Middle East after 2012 and become 'citizens' of Islamic State. Many of these men had lived in Sydney's south-west, just a short drive from Holsworthy Barracks where I conducted my first interviews for *The Commando.*

I ended up writing a book about the commando who had been deployed with PTSD into Iraq then took his own life, about the battle for Mosul and Iraq, and about the Australian enemy that the Australian special forces faced.

The book, *Mosul: Australia's secret war inside the ISIS caliphate*, ended up being a book about violence as a tool for power and control, as well as a book about legacy and the Rubicon (or decisive) moments in life, obvious to Julius Caesar in the moment, but only recognised by most of us in retrospect.

The soldiers I wrote about in *Mosul*, and most of the Australian jihadi, all came to Iraq by way of a total institution, which is an environment in which an individual loses control of their movement, dress, language and, to a certain extent, thought, with media access and communication with people outside that environment limited. There, the soldiers and jihadi were subject to a process called resocialisation, used to change the values, beliefs and norms of an individual.

For the soldiers, their first total institution was the Army Recruit Training Centre in Kapooka where, for eighty days, every soldier in the ADF is trained. According to a University of Tasmania and University of Deakin research paper, this initial training is designed to: 'promote the willing and systematic subordination of one's own individual desires and interests to those of one's unit and, ultimately, country.'

Recruits come into Kapooka as 'red tabs', and are considered as though they are of little worth, to the army and themselves. The red tab period is more concerned with desocialisation than resocialisation; that is, destroying the value systems of the candidate. This is something more easily attained when the candidate is younger. Recruits are yelled at and denigrated, regardless of how effectively they conduct the assigned tasks, and they're made to feel disoriented or worthless. Recruits are denied contact with people outside of Kapooka who may orient them or see them as worthy.

Training is built each week around values, be they courage, respect or integrity. These values are not investigated philosophically as subjective or migratory ideas, but as absolutes and defined by their service to the military.

After three weeks, the recruits become 'blue tabs' and are given more responsibility and it's suggested they have more worth. The yelling subsides. There is live fire weapons training, and the history of the Australian military is taught, from an insular perspective. The 'blue tabs' then become 'gold tabs', but before they do, they go through an essential moment of military resocialisation. Perhaps the most essential moment. The last day the recruits spend as a 'blue tab' is 'Bayo Day', when recruits attach long, sharp knives to dummy rifles and then aggressively attack humanoid figures.

This training is conducted by both recruits in Kapooka and officers training in Canberra and is considered an essential skill, the mastering of which is necessary for the continuation of an army career. This is not because it's likely modern Australian soldiers would be involved in a bayonet charge but because, as Richard Kohn, a professor of military history at the University of North Carolina at Chapel Hill, was reported as telling a United States newspaper: 'Bayonet training is, in short, used to undo socialization – to basically try to mitigate or eradicate the reluctance of human beings to kill each other.'

For most of the Australian jihadi featured in *Mosul*, their total institution was not a mosque where, in Australia, only moderate and relatively moderate forms of Islam are taught, but small clubs and prayer rooms. There, an insular social and ethical framework was established, and for many they were also introduced to a process that would help them kill.

Many were shown violent imagery. First, they were shown photos or videos of Sunni Muslims, often women and children, killed by Western forces in Iraq or Afghanistan or their partner forces which, in the case of Iraq, were often Shi'ites.

Later, many were shown videos of 'righteous kills' against Western or Shi'ite forces, explained as retribution. These videos were often packaged with heroic imagery and religious music.

These jihadi left Australia having been told they had a moral allowance to kill but also a legal allowance, not, of course, under Australian and international law, but under religious law. It was stressed to them that they could kill kufr or non-believers but also Muslims that they had chosen to ex-communicate in a process called takfiri.

The most affecting total environment for both the jihadi and the Australian soldiers was, of course, the fight itself.

Nothing is more radicalising than war and, for the Australian jihadi, this process was turbocharged by the realisation that there was no coming back to Australia.

One such jihadi was a man named Mohammad Baryalei, someone who I'd known very slightly when I first moved to Sydney from Perth.

I'd lived then on Darlinghurst Road, across the road from a strip club where Baryalei worked as a spruiker. I could see him sometimes from a small bedroom window, trying to lure people into a premises that offered drinks and a show, but also famously cocaine and prostitutes.

After a series of mental health episodes, Baryalei became religious and then started his process of radicalisation. In Syria, he was tasked with organising a terrorist atrocity in Sydney.

While working on *Mosul*, I discovered that, in concert with the Australian special forces war-fighting element, an SASR element had also been tracking Australians in ISIS territory. I also discovered that, after Baryalei's conversations were intercepted and his location identified, a lethal strike against Baryalei was approved by Prime Minister Tony Abbott.

Almost all of the Australian men who joined ISIS were killed as the caliphate crumbled, the euphemism 'killed in the fighting' being applied to each death. I think it likely most of those men were targeted by Australian forces and their death sentences approved in Canberra.

Apart from the killing of Baryalei, confirmed to me by Tony Abbott himself, none of the suspected assassinations have been confirmed by the Australian Government, with the closest being Peter Dutton's comments made after reports Khaled Sharrouf had been killed with his two prepubescent sons.

'If he returned to our country, he would be a significant threat to the Australian public,' Dutton said, adding later: 'Sharrouf and his wife took their children into a war zone. If they have been killed, what other outcome would they expect?'

These suspected killings, and the reluctance to bring Australian women and children back home, can be seen as a recognition by the Australian Government of the indelible change that can occur in circumstances as extreme as those found in Iraq and Syria in the Islamic State years.

Such a recognition of damage done to those Australians who went to places like Iraq to work against Australian interests would only make more galling the disregard of the damage done to those who went to places like Iraq, and more notably Afghanistan, in what the government claimed was in the Australian national interest.

A 2012 Dutch study published in the *Proceedings of the National Academy of Sciences of the United States of America* looked at the brains and cognition of Dutch soldiers who had deployed into Uruzgan, Afghanistan, where Australian soldiers also operated.

Using neuropsychological tests and fMRI scans, the study tested the brains and behaviour of the Dutch soldiers before their deployments, establishing a baseline, then conducted the same tests immediately after the soldiers returned to the Netherlands.

Researchers found that, for most soldiers, the prefrontal cortex, the frontal lobe area that regulates planning and personality expression, had appreciably changed after deployment; so, too, the midbrain, an area that's associated with the regulation of movement, vision, hearing and alertness. The researchers also found that, immediately after deployment, the soldiers' ability to complete complicated, non-combat-related tasks had been degraded.

Eighteen months later, the researchers revisited their subjects, again using neuropsychological tests and fMRI scans. They found that, in most cases, the subjects' brains seemed to have returned to the pre-deployment state but, the researchers warned, not completely.

The study found that 'these results suggest that the human brain can largely recover ... supporting the view that neural plasticity in response to prolonged stress is adaptive' but they noted that they had found structural changes in the soldiers' brains, including degradation in the neural connecters between the midbrain and the prefrontal cortex. The study noted that these were 'long-term changes within the mesofrontal network (middle and front part of the brain), that may increase the vulnerability to subsequent stressors and lead to long-lasting cognitive deficits.'

In layperson's terms, the brains of these Dutch soldiers adapted to the environment in Afghanistan, which was violent and dangerous. Civilian tasks and emotions were immaterial, and they were deprioritised so that focus could be migrated to survival. Immediately after deployment, the effects of reprioritisation persisted, but after a year and half of normal Dutch life, the effects had largely reversed themselves. But not completely. The paper recognises that the Dutch soldiers were presenting as the same people they'd been before deployment, but fMRI scanning and historical understanding suggests that may not be the case, and that they may not be as able to deal with further stressors as well as they would have before being deployed.

The finding of the Dutch studies are generally in line with what's known about how stress can affect the brain. It's been long established that the human brain has evolved to change structurally and psychologically when in an instance of extreme stress, which it perceived as existential. Nerve growth is usually decreased in some areas of the brain and some functions like memory function can become limited, so that energy and effort can be redirected to the brain's fight or flight mechanisms.

Following this period of chronic stress, the energy dedicated to fight or flight mechanisms in the brain are deprioritised and energy is dedicated to rewiring and repairing the areas in the brain affected by that stress. This is a period in which there can be significant nerve growth in some areas of the brain.

Afterwards, in most instances, the brain will return to the state it was before the stressor arrived. In some instances, there may have been neurological change during the nerve growth period, which may have been positive. This is believed to be one of the elements involved in post-traumatic growth, a little understood phenomenon in which trauma acts as a catalyst for positive change.

The Dutch study of soldiers deployed to Afghanistan is not a perfect study to understand the experience of Australian soldiers, however, especially not Australian special forces soldiers.

Although the Dutch and Australian soldiers were mostly in Uruzgan, the two forces had very different roles. The Dutch, for instance, largely refused to be involved with the US kill/capture program, a program the Australian special forces were heavily involved in. The largest difference between the two militaries was the frequency with which the Australian special forces deployed to Afghanistan.

The Dutch study only looked at soldiers who had deployed to Afghanistan once, an instance that was rare in the small Australian special forces community. The first Australian special forces soldiers were deployed to Afghanistan in October 2001 and the last in August 2021, to help extract allies and Australian citizens during the fall of Kabul.

From 2005 to 2014, there was a near permanent Australian special forces presence in Afghanistan and, in the high-tempo period, some soldiers conducted eight or more combat deployments to Afghanistan. There is no study available on the effects of such exposure to combat.

The effects are probably profound.

Nerve depletion that follows combat without the relief of nerve growth may affect brain functions permanently and Australian operators may have long-term damage to their memory, visuospatial function, word fluency and the speed that they process information. There may have been long-term emotional damage due to the neurological damage also. Sometimes, this dysregulation and damage can be reversed, but not always. Some brain systems, when overclocked, do not return to their previous state after repeated incident of chronic stress.

I wrote *Mosul* quickly and with a fire under me. I'd spent so much of my career doing work I thought unimportant, but this book felt important to me and quite personal.

I felt that the soldiers in Special Operations Command were abused, especially the sergeant who had taken his own life. With the tempo with which Australia's special forces soldiers were deployed into war zones, the soldiers were in danger of suffering debilitating brain damage akin to a neurological disease or even a stroke.

I thought there should have been a concerted effort to screen Australian soldiers who may have been in danger of suffering permanent physical or psychological damage due to their service. While writing *Mosul*, I found that there been no such effort, and not just that, I had been told that health waivers, especially mental health waivers, were issued so that SOCOMD could stay combat effective in Afghanistan and Iraq.

The other issue that drove me had less to do with the Iraq deployments and more with Afghanistan.

Some elements of Australia's war in Afghanistan were immoral, which affected Afghans and Australians.

A few months after the release of *Mosul*, I received a call from an officer of the New South Wales Coronial Court, asking me to provide the court with a copy of the book.

Coronial proceedings into the death of the sergeant who had been 'chasing the action too long' were about to start and the court officer had been informed that a number of the barristers and solicitors had recently read the book. The court would like a copy.

I was happy to provide a book and to take up the officer's invitation to sit in for some of the testimony, even though I knew it would be confronting to walk into a courtroom and see copies of my book there.

In charge of proceedings was a Deputy State Coroner named Harriet Grahame, and in her opening address she welcomed the soldier's family, explaining that, while some of what was to happen in the courtroom would be difficult for them, ultimately she hoped the experience would be useful and perhaps even something approaching cathartic.

The proceedings were fascinating. By their nature, coronial inquests are not adversarial, like most legal proceedings are. There is no case being presented at the beginning of a coronial inquest, as there is in any criminal or civil court. There are no sides. A coronial inquest starts with a blank page and from it testimony is added. The result of a coronal inquest is a report of what happened, what may have been done and what should be done in the future to avoid more death.

A coronial inquest is like a form of fact-finding that every journalist would dream of being able to undertake. Witnesses are called and, with the coercive powers endowed in the coroner, those witness must appear and must truthfully answer the questions asked of them.

Usually, witnesses appearing in coronial inquests are less combative than in other court proceedings. Usually, they want to help, and with hearsay allowed and their testimony unable to be used in further criminal or civil proceedings, they can usually say their piece more completely than in other court proceedings.

To fear the coroner is to fear the truth. In this instance, the Australian Defence Force feared the coroner, bringing to proceedings easily the largest legal team, partially to protect national security, but I think primarily to protect the reputation of Special Operations Command and the officers therein, and to limit further investigation and potential legal exposure.

Both of the commando's deployments to Iraq after his hospitalisation for PTSD were investigated, with a particular focus on his last deployment, which happened a few months before he took his own life.

I had discovered that the commando had been drinking heavily before the deployment, and on deployment, and that he had expressed a death wish to colleagues. I also found that the commando had arranged to conduct a mission with US Green Berets in Islamic State heartland, attempting to retrieve the body of a US pilot killed in a fight with insurgents. I had been told that the commando had gone out on the mission without body armour and that there were fears he may instigate a gunfight in which he could die. I found that when the mission was completed without a shot being fired, the commando went into a spiral of mental health decline.

At the start of the inquest, Defence flatly denied that the Australian commando had been involved in the Green Beret mission. Later, the Defence legal team was forced to change that position saying that it was 'possible'. This change complicated Defence's position that the soldier's deployment to Iraq to fight Islamic State wasn't something that was likely to create or exacerbate trauma.

Two key witnesses appearing in the inquest were SOCOMD officers who had signed waivers allowing the commando to deploy, despite Joint Health Command categorically stating pre-deployment that the soldier's 'extensive psychological and alcohol dependence history, ongoing stressors … places (him) at high risk of deterioration while deployed'.

One witness was a lieutenant colonel named in court as AF. This man was stern in his look and manner, and gave testimony that appeared to me to verge on being supercilious. He gave evidence that he chose to intervene to deploy the commando because it was in his own 'best interest'.

'I thought his self-worth was intrinsically linked to the company and the company deploying without him would have a detrimental effect,' he said.

The lieutenant colonel later testified that he had not taken any training modules on PTSD, and had no training on the effects of PTSD, nor its causes.

'It was one of the lowest risk of trauma of any of his deployments,' he argued. 'You can find trauma in Sydney.'

My reporting found that the commando had been deployed to al-Taqaddum airbase, on the outskirts of Ramadi, a city that was occupied by Islamic State and liberated at huge human and material cost. The fighting was constant outside al-Taqaddum and the airbase was rocketed several times. While it is true the Australians weren't going door to door, the Iraqis they worked with were and were killed with metronomic regularity. Not to mention the body retrieval mission, that AF testified he knew nothing about.

Ultimately, the officer accepted no responsibility, saying that the commando knew suicide was 'unacceptable' and that, if anything, he had 'failed the army'.

While the testimony of the SOCOMD officers was telling, the evidence that I thought most damned the army, the command and the war in Afghanistan was that of Dr Muhmmad Malik, a psychiatrist who had treated the commando as an inpatient in April 2017, before the soldier took his own life.

Dr Malik was brought in both as a personal and expert witness, speaking about PTSD generally and about the commando's PTSD, which he testified had a specific aspect.

The doctor said the soldier was primarily suffering from a moral injury, meaning the soldier could not reconcile his moral outlook with his memories and actions. Dr Malik noted in his testimony that the commando could not suffer such a mental injury unless he maintained a moral code that he felt had been breached by his own actions.

Dr Malik said that one of the first things the commando said to him was this: 'I've killed so many people, I cannot live with myself, I have killed innocents.'

Messages between the commando and his sister were offered at the inquest and one read: 'It just hurts that my life-long dream and my dream job is the very thing that destroyed me.'

A recent Australian study published in the *International Journal of Mental Health Nursing* noted that:

> Military service fundamentally breaks down a person's existing moral schema and replaces it with a military system of values, beliefs, behaviours and relationships that all function to support the completion of military objectives ... When we accept these transgressions, however pragmatically (for survival, for instance), we sacrifice a piece of our moral integrity.

Military service involves a sort of moral escrow in which the Defence Force and the government retains some of the soldier's moral integrity for the duration of the member's service, as the soldier's agency will be limited while serving and they must follow orders and perform tasks as they are trained to do.

In a democracy, a tacit promise exists, too, between soldier and state, that the military and government will protect the moral integrity that's in escrow and will not direct a soldier to commit acts that are immoral, nor train them in immoral acts.

I believed that compact had been broken and that some soldiers I'd interviewed were suffering moral injuries, a dangerous phenomenon described by Tyler Boudreau in *The Massachusetts Review*:

> Moral injury is about the damage done to our moral fiber when transgressions occur by our hands, through our orders, or with our connivance. When we accept these transgressions, however pragmatic (for survival, for instance), we sacrifice a piece of our moral integrity.

The wars in Afghanistan and both wars in Iraq had been undertaken with the connivance of all of us. The forty-one Australians killed in combat, many of the 1273 Australian soldiers and former soldiers who had died by self-harm since 2001, many of the 11,000 Afghans killed by the Australian special forces, the injuries, mental anguish, money spent, degradation of military capacity and the way the wars may have affected the Australian polity were on one side of a ledger and, on the other was ... what? The destruction of al-Qaeda, the destruction of the Taliban, peace in Iraq?

I was so frustrated by what I'd learned, what had been deliberately hidden from the public during the wars, and how there was little or no other media that seemed to represent the truth about the wars as it was being explained to me. I managed to finish *Mosul*, at least in part, because I was driven to address my own minor moral injury, feeling it as a citizen and someone who had unique access to the story of the wars.

When I started writing *Mosul*, I often found myself overawed by the audacity of the project. There was so much to the story, and so much context required. This was a story about national secrets, a dense bureaucracy, trauma, psychology, geopolitics and war, and the person trying to wrap his head around it all was a former high school dropout and *Ralph* goofball with a broken brain.

I felt my broken brain often when writing *Mosul*. I'd have a Word document open and surrounding it would be maps, transcriptions, news articles, white papers, photographs and combat footage and it would feel as though it wasn't only the RAM on my computer being tested.

Sometimes, at my desk, my basic sentence structure would break down and I'd lose the most elementary words. Sometimes I'd find myself rewriting one sentence hundreds of times, while googling synonyms for simple words that had escaped me like 'transgression' or 'obituary'. Sometimes I'd barely be able to order coffee and lunch in a break, overwhelmed and overthinking the syntax of my request.

In those times, on those days that I call my 'strokey days', I'd leave the house conspiring to quit the project, telling myself that I couldn't possibly be the right person to tell this story.

When walking down on the beach or along the cliffs, or along largely empty but familiar streets, I found a mantra I used to force me back to my desk, and something that's been useful away from my writing desk also.

You can't do everything but you can do something.

You can't do everything but you can do something.

I think I managed to finish that book because of that mantra, and because of the strange and wonderful times I found myself in. I wrote *Mosul* in 2020, when all of us were forced hard to think about our own moral schema, and what we owed to the community. It was a year in which all of our lives changed, and mine more than most.

Chapter 14

and there you were

In 2020, so many plans were blown apart and then reassembled. My plans were blown apart and reassembled, yet it wasn't Covid that changed the trajectory of my life, but a beautiful actress named Claire.

I'd known Claire van der Boom for about twenty years, but not well. Some time in the early 2000s, when Claire was studying acting at the National Institute of Dramatic Art and I was working as a music journalist, she and I smushed ourselves together one night, after we ended up at the same beach house. Perhaps it wasn't love at first sight, but it was certainly something instantaneous. When the weekend ended, we de-smushed. Such was the nature of relationships at that age.

Claire finished her studies and went on to work as an actress in Australia and then the United States, in film, TV and also on stage in New York. We maintained the most tenuous connection on social media until, near the end of 2019, we reconnected.

Claire claims it was me who messaged her on Instagram and I insist it was her. Either way, we started chatting about the fact that she was leaving Los Angeles and coming back to Australia. To Bondi, no less.

I was the one who suggested that I welcome her to the neighbourhood with a drink and we agreed to meet up. On a Saturday afternoon, we met at a dive bar on Bondi Road.

We shared bloody marys and I was at pains to try to stay breezy, but I was nervous. In Claire, in her manner, grace and history, I saw something I very much wanted to share. I already wanted to be with her. I wanted to know her.

After a couple of drinks, I was glad that I had booked a reservation for a chic restaurant across the road. Just in case. As the sun fell and the day cooled, she agreed to come over to the restaurant. We ate blackened fish and drank margaritas. We talked about life's little stuff and big. We were again smushed together and this time we stayed smushed.

Claire and I saw each other the next day, then the next and so on. My depth of feeling for her only grew as we enjoyed Sydney's late summer together, mostly in Bondi but also in Chinatown, at the national park, at theatres and cinemas. We moved around on my motorbike under the sun and moon. The wind whipped us but the bike's engine warmed us. Her arms were wrapped around my belly. That's joy.

This woman had an understanding of life beyond explanation, which is what it is to have an artist's heart. I was in awe of that. Claire is simply beautiful, skin and soul. I couldn't believe that I'd found her, and was even more disbelieving that she'd chosen me. Then, after sharing Claire with the city for a few weeks, all of a sudden, the world closed down. And we were with each other almost exclusively. Covid ramped up and the city locked down. Claire and I were stuck together in the beautiful frozen here and now.

We baked bread, danced in our lounge room, spent days in bed and fell deeply in love.

At the time, the deadline for my book on Mosul was rushing towards me, no longer a dot on the horizon but a rabid animal demanding to be fed.

My planned trip to Mosul, Baghdad and al-Hawl camp (where some Australians are still interned at the time of writing) was cancelled. That could have been a disaster but Covid meant pretty much everyone in the world was at home and available on Zoom.

The book didn't end up being what I imagined it would be, which is not to say it was worse or better, just different.

I limped and tumbled over the line of my *Mosul* deadline, having woken some days at 4 am to write in the frigid dark and then emerge from my office in the afternoon blinking uncomfortably like a bear coming out of his den at the end of winter. Thankfully, when my eyes adjusted to the light, Claire was still there.

Claire's industry came out of the Covid hole, not timidly but hungrily. Everyone had been bingeing TV and movies while at home, so demand in film and television programming had only grown while supply had been throttled. With the United States suffering a Covid deluge of death and disease all through 2020, Australia became something of a safe haven and hosted all kinds of productions, including a low-budget thriller shooting at a resort in far-north Queensland starring Claire van der Boom as its lead.

While *Mosul* was being printed, I travelled with Claire to the tropics. There, I learned even more about the woman I had fallen for. Claire had grown up in Broome, and the place still had a piece of her heart. At Cable Beach, she found a foundational part of herself, like the part I found at Cottesloe Beach after moving from Canberra to Perth.

One day, we went into Port Douglas and bought prawns off the deck of the trawler that caught them. As we ate, Claire talked about her family. Her dad, Pieter, had been a Dutch merchant marine in the 1960s, finding work as a pearl diver in Broome, and her mum, Judith, was a fun and adventurous Kiwi who made it to Broome by way of much of the world.

The family had settled in Perth, but when Pieter and Jude's marriage dissolved, Pieter went back to Broome. That's where he is to this day.

The resort Claire's film was being shot at sat on a beautiful, deserted stretch of sand called Oak Beach, which Claire and I walked up and down each day chatting about this or that. One day on that beach, Claire told me that her brother PJ would have been celebrating his fortieth birthday that day, but he'd been killed in a car accident nearly twenty years earlier.

She drew a message to her brother in the sand, which she photographed and sent to their mother. The tide came to wash the message away and Claire cried in my arms. Claire's grief is still indelibly part of her and became part of our relationship also. I think of PJ often.

Claire and I resumed our glorious, loving carefree lives together in Sydney for a little while and then, the week before *Mosul* came out, our lives changed drastically again.

I'd been playing Xbox when it happened. Claire walked into my apartment, pulled the headphones from my head, slumped herself on the couch next to me, thrust a pregnancy test in front of me and kissed my cheek. Of the hundreds of thoughts that were running through my head, one was paramount: I was incredibly lucky that this was happening with Claire, and so too was this baby.

For both Claire and me, the primary sorrow of the pandemic was our inability to go west as all four of our parents were stuck in Western Australia, a state that had decided to divorce itself from the rest of the country with the backing of the state's government, media, populace and primary industry, mining.

In November 2020, we were finally able to travel to Perth. We were planning to tell everyone after our two weeks in quarantine, but dietary requirements and loud morning (all-day) sickness forced us to prematurely tell Claire's mum, who we were staying with. We had to tell her from a socially distanced balcony but Jude positively vibrated out of her skin at the news and her husband Colin was happy in a beautiful way. Their enthusiasm about the news was matched when Pieter, who was in Perth for a visit, was told by way of a re-engineered Kong Foo Sing fortune cookie, a nod to the long happy evenings their family had spent at Broome's Chinese restaurant in the early 1990s.

My mum's response was muted, which I think was primarily due to shock. I was delighted that our midwife called Claire while my mum was visiting, so all three of us could learn that we would be welcoming a girl into the world. Mum can have a façade that's hard to crack sometimes, but I know her nuances well enough to recognise how quickly she loved Claire and how excited she was for the child who was coming into our lives.

It was only after we'd been released from quarantine that we had the opportunity to tell my dad, who was not well enough to drive from Mandurah to the Perth balcony from which we gave everyone else the news.

Life started throwing heavy blows at Dad in September 2018. The first was the death of his friend Steve Morgan. Steve had been battling cancer and died that year, while Dad was away in the United Kingdom.

I flew to Melbourne to attend Steve's funeral in Dad's stead and it all felt too close – music from Bob Dylan, Van Morrison and Etta James played and the service ended with 'The Irish Blessing'. It could have been Dad's funeral.

I gave my love to Steve's family, especially Di, and left, reporting back to Dad on the phone later. The devastation in his voice was absolute.

Steve had meant so much to Dad, and when I hung up I felt an immense gratitude for my shaggy, long-striding tattooed uncle. Dad's relationship with Steve was the only place where Dad had been able to give and receive love as a teen and young man. I imagined Dad would have been a very different man if Steve had been absent from his formative years.

Steve's death devastated Dad's spirit and, shortly afterwards, his body also started to fail him. He started to lose vision in one eye, and hearing in his remaining good ear. He had problems with his balance and he suffered nose bleeds.

On the phone, these problems were mentioned in an off-hand way, if at all, and most of the information I got about Dad's physical state was from my sister. Neither of us knew exactly what was going on, but we both feared something serious may be happening. Dad steadfastly refused to take on any information he didn't want to, and he didn't want to know he had cancer.

We'd known for a while that a shadow behind Dad's nose had shown up on X-rays but we were told it was nothing. Even when the definitive cancer diagnosis came, Dad downplayed it. He refused to admit that he had cancer because 'doctors had used another word that I can't remember right now, not cancer'.

Radiotherapy took Dad's moustache and he became bare-faced for the first time since he was a teenager. I grew a sympathy moustache, but I didn't wear it as well as he did.

Some of the later months of 2019 were tough on my dad. He was very ill and intermittently confused. He became spectrally thin but maintained that the whole incident would soon be behind him.

I was in Perth for Christmas in 2019, and for the birthday of my eldest niece, Audrey. We all spent time together, Dad coming to a public pool for a party and sitting next to Mum as my sister's three daughters splashed around like angelic maniacs. Dad seemed to be much improved. It was a lovely moment. Our family were all gathered in what ended up being our last time together.

In January 2020, I went back to Bondi hoping Dad was getting better. And then I reconnected with Claire. My family lived their lives in Western Australia and I lived mine in Bondi.

One rainy Saturday morning, I was thinking of Dad while I was walking up and down Bondi Road, and he called me. We spoke about a television show he was watching and I asked about the ongoing mystery that was his medical situation. He gave me some rare, solid and unqualified knowledge that a doctor had imparted to Dad, which he had retained and now passed on to me. Dad was dying. The manner in which Dad gave me the news didn't suggest bad news, but of course it was. Dad said he'd been told that it may be years before the end, but the end was inevitable.

I had no idea how to react, and only reflected the energy that Dad had sent. He seemed happy. He was in a different stage of treatment and the months that he'd endured, of illness and spotty cognition and memory, were seemingly behind him. He was dying but he was at least more himself.

He didn't want to talk about his cancer. He'd delivered the news he had to, and just wanted to chitchat, so chitchat we did. At the end of the conversation, I told him that I'd come to visit him as soon as I could then I told him I loved him. I hung up and I cried and cried and cried, and cried some more.

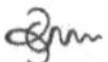

After finishing quarantine in Perth, Claire and I went to Mandurah to stay with Dad and Marlene. We sat at their dining table in front of hot teas and I told Dad I was going to be a father. He was so happy. Dad bubbled, levitated and hosted gloriously. He told stories about his life I'd never heard, finding in Claire a willing audience. Dad listened too, wanting to know about Claire's life and work, stoking again a childhood fire for talented and beautiful actresses.

Dad usually exhausted quickly, but not that night. As Claire and I went to bed tired, Dad and Marlene were still on a tear, opening a bottle of red wine they'd been saving. Claire and I giggled in the dark of Dad's guest bedroom as Dad and Marlene's comments vibrated through the thin walls. Dad was in love with Claire also.

We went back to Perth and the next day Dad sent me a picture of a tall, cold Guinness, something Dad used to do from time to time. Marlene sent me a message telling me they went out for dinner, something they'd not done for some time. She told me Dad was still on a happy cloud.

A few months later, Claire and I were staying with Dad and Marlene. It was 7 January 2021. Claire was sleeping late, gripped as she was for much of the pregnancy with morning sickness, and I was up with an instant coffee. My Dad and I were watching what looked a lot like a frontal assault on the US Capitol Building.

Thousands of people, many wearing red MAGA hats and Trump shirts, were battling with an overwhelmed police presence. I watched with amazement but also horror. If I was a senator stuck in the Capitol, I'd want the mass mobilisation of a relieving force. This force may be military. I feared what the United States may look like after dozens or perhaps hundreds of MAGA Republicans were killed by American soldiers. I also feared the small chance some soldiers might decide they had a common cause with those who were killed.

My mind spun in the way that it had when I sat in a pub in central Sydney watching lower Manhattan burn twenty years before. Where do we go from here? Meanwhile, Dad just laughed.

'They should do what the Chinese do: take them out and shoot them,' he said.

This was a refrain that I'd heard a few times from Dad over the last few years and it always made me wince. Before I started working on *The Commando* and *Mosul*,

I'd only seen a few, relatively antiseptic pictures of people who'd been shot, but since then I'd seen a lot. Many vets I worked with retained a cache of graphic images that were sometimes shared with me. Sometimes it may feel like we live in a culture saturated with violence, but we don't. Not yet. In battlefield images, there is another level of brutality that can be seen: bodies that look like butchery, heads opened like fruit, faces spread in two places.

When Dad spoke about people being shot, I thought about those images. I also thought about how my dad had once had such a honed and argumentative sense of right and wrong. I thought of his changing media diet and his intermittent citation of Andrew Bolt, Sky News and his hate of watching 'the ladies at the ABC'.

I knew it was just a figure of speech. I knew it was also an imposition of order when disorder and complication ruled his life now, even on a cellular level. I shouldn't have cared and yet I did.

I decided to write one last book about Afghanistan. The difficult one. The biggest one. The one that I could never have written had I not written the others before. It was a story that had been suggested to me in whispers while working on my other military books. It was the story of Australian soldiers taking people out and sometimes detaining them, or sometimes shooting them.

Chapter 15

sunrise, sunset

Claire and I (but mostly Claire) had plans for our baby girl to be eased into this world with fit balls, soft music, candles and all that. She had other ideas. One minute, there were dawn contractions, the next, an insistence from a midwife that we get to hospital immediately.

On the drive to the Mater Hospital and on the ward there, things went very quicky then very slowly. Our daughter was coaxed out eventually, though; a screaming pink bundle of dough the prize of all of Claire's incredible work. For days, we fed her, changed her and sent her here and there for tests with no name, just a blank space on the whiteboard in our hospital room.

We tried some names but they were decidedly not hers. She was Poppy; we knew it the moment we wrote it up on the board. Poppy Johanna Mckelvey. PJ. Claire liked the idea of bringing a PJ into the world, and I did too. Poppy the flower, Poppy the symbol, Poppy our daughter.

We went home, and there were some moments in those early weeks that were just so beautiful; her tiny belly against my scar as she stared at me, Claire dancing her to sleep in the lounge room as Bowie played. On rare occasions, when we had cause to leave the apartment, we did, all three of us seeing the world anew.

Some moments were very hard, though. I found the baby's crying difficult. Of course, I knew all babies cry a lot in the first few months, and I knew that my baby would be no different, but that didn't stop me from, deep in the night when she was crying out for something neither Claire nor I could give, privately spiralling.

I sometimes imagined that, with her tiny life yet to be filled with minutia, memories and relationships, she saw through the clutter of life and into the maw of existence. Sometimes, when she cried, I imagined she knew even the tenderest of embraces would not warm a giant, cold universe. Sometimes I was taken back to the worst parts of my young adulthood.

I was overwhelmed by stress and think now that I may have already been grieving the years my dad and Poppy were not going to spend together.

In the latter months of 2021, Dad started walking with a stick. He experienced a lot of pain. A shoulder injury first bothered him, then frustrated him, then it became agony. It was later diagnosed as a break, not from impact, just the brittleness of bones post-treatment. It was confronting to understand that this bone would never heal.

Affected by pain and medications to confront that pain, Dad's cognition came and went. Sometimes he was as he'd always been and sometimes it was as though he was lost in a mist. I wanted to be with him and I wanted to bring Poppy to him. Claire wanted to be with her family, too. Time was moving differently for both of us now and both of us urgently wanted to go to Western Australia, but it had never been harder to do so.

Western Australia was still stubbornly resisting incorporation with the rest of the country. Despite Covid cases all but disappearing in New South Wales, and despite the pandemic now being more than eighteen months old, Western Australia had support for insularity and a failing quarantine infrastructure, so there was no pathway for entry except through an expensive hotel quarantine program that you needed to be invited into.

Ostensibly, there was a provision for compassionate entry into quarantine and so I arranged for Dad's doctors to send diagnostic papers to me so they could be sent to the Western Australian police.

It was confronting to see the reality of Dad's prognosis and then monumentally frustrating to have our application to enter quarantine refused time and time again by an automated system that was designed to be impenetrable. It was a stressful time.

Eventually we were approved and we left quarantine on my mum's birthday. We went to the beach, ate fish and chips and, as the sun set over the Indian Ocean, my sister, my mum and Claire chased around happy nieces who were excited to welcome a cousin they called 'Baby Boom'.

She was a gift to us all. When we took her to see my dad, he wasn't in great shape.

He was even thinner than I'd expected, and less mobile and less energetic. I wanted for Poppy all the fun that her cousins had experienced with my dad. I wanted her to bask in the surprising energy and capacity he had for imaginative and silly play.

It didn't happen. It was never going to happen. Dad could only hold Poppy in his lap for a few minutes. He was suffering physically. He seemed in decent spirits, but he didn't have the energy nor strength to hold a five-month-old baby.

Dad loved Poppy, that I could tell, but he was tired and he was in pain and he was dying, which he wanted to do on his terms.

By the time we were leaving Perth, then Western Australian Premier Mark McGowan had announced that the border to the eastern states would soon open so I left my dad, telling him that I loved him and that I'd see him again soon. I thought we had more time. Dad may have known that we didn't.

After I returned to Sydney, Dad and I chatted, about the Ashes and whatever else was happening in the world. He was still Dad, on the phone and in messages. Then, just before Christmas, the messages and calls ended.

I spoke to my sister and she told me Dad had been overwhelmed by an infection, which was being addressed with powerful antibiotics. Marlene arranged for a nurse to visit them so they could give 'phase one care', which is palliative care but not end-of-life care. Nurses moved Dad to a bed in the front room of his place and there he battled the infection. When Dad was well enough to speak, we spoke. He was groggy, to say the least. When then Premier McGowan announced the border would open on 5 February, I booked flights for us all on that day.

But Dad started to deteriorate and my hope we'd all see Dad again started to disappear. Laura was there with him at the end, and Marlene.

My sister connected me to Dad through a WhatsApp video and, in my little office, I watched him as I worked.

The television was on sometimes, when there was football. A Buddy Holly CD spun around the spool of an old player. Marlene held Dad's hand. Laura held his hand as though trying to keep him here.

I filed for an immediate compassionate entry into Western Australia, where I may have been allowed to enter hotel quarantine and then be escorted to see Dad while wearing full personal protective equipment and stand alone.

As that request groaned through the Western Australian bureaucracy, Dad transitioned into 'phase two care'. Silver Chain nurses tried to keep Dad comfortable, which meant keeping him mostly asleep. When Dad did raise into consciousness, he was panicked. Marlene said it was because the pad under him was full, and it sent him all the way back to those nights in Silverlands, the actor's orphanage, waking in terror as he felt hotness and wetness under the cover.

I'm sure she was right, but when I saw it on my phone, I couldn't help but imagine Dad reciting Dylan Thomas as he did sometimes, when I was a boy.

Rage, rage against the dying of the light.

I watched and I waited and I cried and I sat down and I started to write this book. Over the next few days, all the things that made Dad the man I'd loved seemed to sink into the bed.

Then, very early in the morning of 11 January 2022, my sister called to tell me that Dad's light was gone.

I had told myself that I didn't need to be with Dad at the end, nor did I want to see him before they took his body away. I told myself that it was okay that we'd have a wake weeks after his death. I told myself that my relationship with Dad was all the time we spent together, over four decades, and the details of a few final rituals meant little.

It was when it was announced that the Western Australian border opening was to be delayed indefinitely that I realised how much I needed my family, and how tenuous my grip on sanity had been.

I became overwhelmed and stopped properly functioning. I again became depressive and manic.

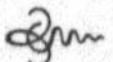

The loss of a loved one can affect the brain significantly. The evolutionarily ancient limbic system, also sometimes known as 'the lizard brain' – an area most associated with fight and flight mechanisms – can go into overdrive after a loss. The stress hormone cortisol is noticeably higher in those who are grieving. Activity in the prefrontal cortex, the part of the brain where more nuanced and reasoned thinking happens, often slows down.

After losing a loved one, a person may also find it more difficult to make decisions that don't relate to existential risk; and their capacity for reason, cognition, creativity and language skills may be limited.

Loss affects the brain in many of the same ways real danger does. In many ways, the brain can see grief as the possibility of death itself. This fact is captured in so many cultures and religions by removing the bereaved from the living world and tenderly caring for them before they can be reintegrated.

In the Jewish faith, the bereaved stay at home for a week and friends and family bring food and sit with them quietly, on low stools. In some Asian cultures, this homebound period is much longer. In dozens of cultures across the world, the bereaved wear dark colours, identifying them as someone who has one foot in our world and one in the next.

Eventually the bereaved come back wholly to the world of the living. Except in rare instances (and more often after a loss that involved a shocking or violent death), the changes in the brain and cortisol levels suffered after a loss revert to a normal state after weeks or months.

This is not where grief ends, however. With cognition and reasoning and memory having returned, a new reality occurs in which the bereaved is wholly alive and the loved one wholly dead.

This is where grief really begins. This is where those who have lost someone must make sense of life, reconcile with the death and find a way to move forward.

We decided to fly to Perth on 5 February anyway, and into the last two-week Covid quarantine that existed on Earth. I really needed my sister and my mum, who had also been sick and hospitalised after Dad's death with a malady the doctors couldn't identify or quite pin down. I needed my family to be with Claire, Poppy and me. I felt in my being the way the body feels it needs food and water.

After two days in quarantine, it was announced that Western Australia was moving immediately into a seven-day quarantine as their own community transmission of Covid was becoming widespread. Initially it was announced that those already in quarantine must complete the fourteen-day exclusion to make administration easier for police, but that announcement only lasted a few rageful hours.

My sister and I helped arrange an unfussy wake for Dad, where there was Guinness and party pies in Dad's backyard with his Mandurah friends. It seemed a small affair to mark the ending of such a life, but it was probably still more than he would have wanted.

Claire, Poppy and I stayed in Perth for nearly two months. We moved in Perth's rhythms: boat rides to Rottnest Island, time on the wide river, the quiet CBD and lots of family time. I went to Cottesloe Beach on many afternoons, with Poppy, Claire and I swimming in calm waters until one of those brilliant sunsets came.

Moving around in the circle of things helped me start to repair. Eventually I took to a desk at Claire's parents' place and threw myself into the last stages of my last book about the war in Afghanistan. I had to finish what I had started.

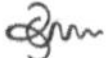

Find Fix Finish: from Tampa to Afghanistan – how Australia's special forces became enmeshed in the US kill/capture program was my longest, most researched, most newsworthy and, I think, best book about the war in Afghanistan.

It bulged with new information about the war and about Australia's secret kill/capture program, which the book posits is the key to understanding Australia's war, thanks to dozens of interviews with key Australian, American, Dutch and Afghan figures, some of whom were on the tools and others who were strategic figures or even heads of state.

It explains the nature of Australia's war in Afghanistan and why and how it went so wrong. It's also far from being the last word on the war required.

The book asked more questions than it answered, a quality that it shared with the defamation trial initiated by Ben Roberts-Smith. There was a lot more to say about the war and its prosecution, but it didn't need to be said by me.

In that lift with Ben Roberts-Smith, I realised I should let the war in Afghanistan go. I knew I'd have to let my dad go, too. When preparing to welcome Poppy into the world, I knew other changes in my life had to be made. I had to get on top of the compulsions, curiosities and defence mechanisms that had driven my life. I had to put to rest the idea that figuring out my life was such an important endeavour. I needed all my energy for my daughter.

While writing *Find, Fix, Finish*, I realised I needed to start a season of letting go. This book in your hands was written in the service of ending that season.

Now a new season can begin.

epilogue

Poppy, you're approaching twenty-two months old as I finish editing this book. We've recently returned from your first family holiday, to Vietnam. There, we took you to the Thang Long Water Puppet Theatre in Hanoi where, four times a day, a company of traditional musicians and puppeteers perform essentially the same small scenes depicting Vietnamese folk stories that were created by bored farmers in flooded fields almost a thousand years before.

We bought tickets in the front row and were ushered into the theatre a few minutes before the show was set to start. As the theatre filled behind us, your mum and I thought we'd made a terrible mistake. You didn't want to sit, you wanted to stand. You didn't want to stand, you wanted to run. You wanted to yell and then, as the house lights dimmed, a group of musicians in traditional Vietnamese dress walked onto stage and you groaned.

After a note of general mild discontent when a single light pierced the auditorium, illuminating a woman preparing to strike her first note on her đàn bầu, you roared out a fart whose volume was in no way commensurate with your size. I tried not to giggle (and failed) as I looked at the doorway to the lobby. Perhaps, I thought, we could watch some of the show from there.

Then the music started, which was unusual but very beautiful. The player, a middle-aged woman, concentrated in a way musicians performing the same music four times a day often don't. Poppy, when she started playing, you stared at her and you were quiet.

The rest of the musicians eventually joined her in playing and some small wooden dragons burst from the water, chasing each other up and down the stage, left and right, with fireworks in their mouths. Your hand thrust forward, pointing at the dragons then, looking to Claire and me, then to the people behind us, as though to say: 'Are you all seeing this, too?'

After the dragons came a series of simple four- or five-minute vignettes, many rural peasants chasing or being chased by demons and spirits, absurd violence and implied fornications.

'Punch and Judy,' Claire whispered. Punch and Judy indeed.

You loved it. You were silent and still, except when pointing at the stage in amazement. After each scene, you turned to us and asked for 'more, more, more'. We were happy to pretend we were obliging.

You watched the show in its entirety, captured and still. I watched the show sometimes, and sometimes I looked at the light dancing on your face. I'd always enjoyed taking a moment to look around me to see the faces of the people in an audience to see if they are in the pocket. Same when I see someone deep in a great book. I never got as much pleasure as I did when I watched you, though, Poppy.

This show will be a whole memory for me for the rest of my life, yet it will be mist for you, if at all. It happened, though. It's in there.

The idea of whole memories and mist is something I think of often now I'm a dad, especially when you are still in the 'infantile amnesia' period. I think of all the moments you and I have shared: your head on my shoulder as we walk the streets at dawn, learning how a neighbourhood dog can best be patted, the moment when you fly into my arms when demanding a cuddle. I think of all the private moments I had with my dad, which were lost as conscious memories when we lost him but are still there somewhere. It happened. It all happened. It changed me and it's changing you.

I wonder sometimes whether these innumerable anonymous kindnesses, recognitions, observations and revelations are the true engine of our lives. Not only those that are lost because they happened before our biographical memories start to imprint (usually everything before the age of three), but also because the moment is resigned, as so many are, into the files of the unconscious mind.

So much of this book has been about life's drastic pivots and so much of this book has been about cruelties and damage, which can change a life in single moments, in contrast to kindnesses which often work in bulk.

Poppy, I don't want to end this book that I'm writing for you with bombast, and certainly not cruelty, but with a small kindness. I want to end this book with a đàn bầu singing, a musician caring, a water dragon rising and your eyes growing wide.

I want to end this book with you on my lap, tears in my eyes, my dad on my mind, and your mum's hands holding mine.

select sources

Chapter 3

Birgit Mampe, Angela D Friederici, Anne Christophe & Kathleen Wermke, 'Newborns' Cry Melody is Shaped by Their Native Language', *Current Biology*, 19:23, December 2009, pp 1994–97.

Chapter 4

'Blessed and Cursed by an Extraordinary Memory', NPR, 19 May 2008, www.npr.org/transcripts/90596530.

Chapter 9

Joan Didion, *The White Album*, Simon & Schuster, New York, 1979.

J Marvin Eisenstadt, 'Parental Loss and Genius', *American Psychologist*, 33:3, 1978, pp 211–33.

Chapter 10

George Saunders, *A Swim in a Pond in the Rain*, Random House, New York, 2021.

Norman Mailer, *The Fight*, Little, Brown, Boston, 1975.

'Hunger and malnutrition being driven by climate crisis and conflict in South Sudan', World Food Programme, 3 November 2022, www.wfp.org/news/hunger-and-malnutrition-being-driven-climate-crisis-and-conflict-south-sudan.

Chapter 11

Brian I O'Toole, Tammy Orreal-Scarborough, Deborah Johnston, Stanley V Catts & Sue Outram, 'Suicidality in Australian Vietnam Veterans and Their Partners', *Journal of Psychiatric Research*, 65, June 2015, pp 30–36.

Rachel Yehuda, Nikolaos P Daskalakis, Linda M Bierer, Heather N Bader, Torsten Klengel, Florian Holsboer & Elisabeth B Binder, 'Holocaust Exposure Induced Intergenerational Effects on *FKBP5* Methylation', *Biological Psychiatry*, 80:5, September 2016, pp 372–80.

Gene M Heyman, 'Addiction and Choice: Theory and New Data', *Frontiers in Psychology*, 4:31, May 2013.

Sandra Düzel, Johanna Drewelies, Denis Gerstorf, Ilja Demuth, Elisabeth Steinhagen-Thiessen, Ulman Lindenberger & Simone Kühn, 'Structural Brain Correlates of Loneliness among Older Adults', *Scientific Reports*, 9, September 2019.

Lamya Khoury, Yilang L Tang, Bekh Bradley, Joe F Cubells & Kerry J Ressler, 'Substance Use, Childhood Traumatic Experience, and Posttraumatic Stress Disorder in an Urban Civilian Population', *Depression and Anxiety*, 27:12, December 2010, pp 1077–86.

Sophie Weiner, 'Applying the Addictive Psychology of Slot Machines to App Design', *Fast Company*, 12 May 2015, www.fastcompany.com/3046149/applying-the-addictive-psychology-of-slot-machines-to-app-design.

Chapter 13

John Fox & Bob Pease, 'Military Deployment, Masculinity and Trauma: Reviewing the Connections', *The Journal of Men's Studies*, 20:1, January 2012, pp 16–31.

Anna Mulrine, 'One less skill for soldiers to master at boot camp: bayonet training', *The Christian Science Monitor*, 28 September 2010, www.csmonitor.com/USA/Military/2010/0928/One-less-skill-for-soldiers-to-master-at-boot-camp-bayonet-training.

Dylan Welch & Suzanne Dredge, 'Khaled Sharrouf, Australian terrorist, believed to have been killed in air strike in Syria', ABC News, 16 August 2017, www.abc.net.au/news/2017-08-16/khaled-sharrouf-believed-to-have-been-killed/8812600.

Guido A van Wingen, Elbert Geuze, Matthan WA Caan, Tamás Kozicz, Silvia D Olabarriaga, Damiaan Denys, Eric Vermetten & Guillén Fernández, 'Persistent and Reversible Consequences of Combat Stress on the Mesofrontal Circuit and Cognition', *Proceedings of the National Academy of Sciences of the United States of America*, 109:38, September 2012, pp 15508–13.

Lisa M Shulman, MD, FAAN, 'Healing Your Brain After Loss: How Grief Rewires the Brain', American Brain Foundation, 29 September 2021, www.americanbrainfoundation.org/how-tragedy-affects-the-brain.

Washington University in St Louis, 'Military service, even without combat, can change personality and make vets less agreeable, research suggests', ScienceDaily, 17 February 2012, www.sciencedaily.com/releases/2012/02/120217101908.htm.

Nikki Jamieson, Myfanwy Maple, Dorothy Ratnarajah & Kim Usher, 'Military Moral Injury: A Concept Analysis',

International Journal of Mental Health Nursing, 29:6, November 2020, 1049–66.

Tyler Boudreau, 'The Morally Injured', *The Massachusetts Review*, 52, 2011, pp 746–54.

Australian Institute of Health and Welfare, *Serving and Ex-serving Australian Defence Force Members Who Have Served Since 1985: Suicide Monitoring 2001 to 2019*, Australian Institute of Health and Welfare (cat. no. PHE 290), Canberra, 2021.

acknowledgements

Thanks to Claire, who is half of the world and has all of my heart. And to Mum, to Laura and, of course, to Dad. Thanks to all who have trusted me with their stories over the years, especially to Mark and Deng. Thanks to Vanessa, without whom there would be no book (and maybe no books at all). And thanks to Deonie, Emma and Jeremy, for their help.

hachette
AUSTRALIA

If you would like to find out more about Hachette Australia, our authors, upcoming events and new releases you can visit our website or our social media channels:

hachette.com.au

HachetteAustralia

HachetteAus